Jonathan,

Enjoy Money Mindset,

Money Mindset

Money Mindset

Formulating a Wealth Strategy in the 21st Century

Jacob Gold

WILEY

Published by John Wiley & Sons, Inc., Hoboken, New Jersey.
Published simultaneously in Canada.

For general information on our other products and services or for technical support, please
contact our Customer Care Department within the United States at (800) 762-2974,
outside the United States at (317) 572-3993 or fax (317) 572-4002.

Wiley publishes in a variety of print and electronic formats and by print-on-demand.
Some material included with standard print versions of this book may not be included in
e-books or in print-on-demand. If this book refers to media such as a CD or DVD that
is not included in the version you purchased, you may download this material at http://
booksupport.wiley.com. For more information about Wiley products, visit www.wiley.com.

Library of Congress Cataloging-in-Publication Data:

ISBN 9781119136057 (Hardcover)
ISBN 9781119136071 (ePDF)
ISBN 9781119136064 (ePub)

Printed in the United States of America

10 9 8 7 6 5 4 3 2 1

I dedicate this book to my three children:
Kelvin, Savanna, and Bella.

May the wisdom in this book help fuel
your aspirations in life.

Contents

Contents

Foreword

The everyday investor was not prepared for the Great Recession that shook the world in 2008. And too many have found themselves repeatedly wrong-footed by the markets in the eventful years that have followed; the excessive risk-taking that characterized the precrisis zeitgeist gave way to the hunker-down mentality of the postcrisis period, leaving behind a wide swath of investors whose extreme risk aversion prevented them from participating in the fourth-longest bull market in history.

And while the relentless advance of markets off their 2009 troughs has made it look easy for those with the fortitude to remain fully invested, in truth the world—and the investment environment—has grown more complex, not less. The crisis-entrenched Euro Zone, a doubling down on unconventional monetary policy by global central banks, and ever-evolving geopolitical risks are but a few of the factors giving investors inclined toward skittishness ample justification for their fears.

Fortunately, we have Jacob Gold to help make sense of it all. I've had the pleasure of working closely with Jacob in my capacity as spokesperson for the Voya Global Perspectives program and find myself consistently impressed with his planning and investing acumen. As he did with his 2009 release *Financial Intelligence: Getting Back to Basics after an Economic Meltdown,* Jacob in his new book delivers practical, real-world advice for investors in search of a comprehensive plan for their assets. *Money Mindset: Formulating a Wealth Strategy in the 21st Century* seeks to shape the financial mindset for this young century by drawing a parallel between our nation's rapid ascent toward energy independence and the individual investor's quest for financial independence.

Money Mindset shows readers how to create a plan to grow wealth, protect it, and transfer it to future generations. Jacob advises thinking of the many areas that contribute to a successful retirement—from the various funding sources like pensions, insurance, social security, and retirement savings vehicles to the shifting asset allocation over time—holistically and always in the context of an investor's end game. This latter factor is key and demands of investors an honest, forthright, and realistic assessment of their wants, needs, and objectives, both now and in retirement.

Knowing the risks to accept and manage versus those to transfer can mean the difference between a successful financial plan and one that falls short. Throughout *Money Mindset,* Jacob offers diversification techniques that can help mitigate a portfolio's vulnerability to fickle global markets, while also highlighting the disparate opportunities energy independence may present for a number of sectors, industries, and consumers that maybe don't immediately come to mind.

Jacob's insights and experience make this an important book not only for the general public but for financial professionals as well. As a third-generation wealth manager, planning and investing is, as Jacob says, "somehow embedded in my DNA." A close read of *Money Mindset* will serve anyone without this expertise imprinted in their genetic code.

—Douglas Coté, CFA
Chief Market Strategist
Voya Investment Management
New York, NY

Preface

The beginning of the 21st century in the United States has been economically volatile and quite unpredictable. Crises resulting from the dot-com boom and bust to the real estate bubble and bank crises that fueled the Great Recession to the ever-changing geopolitical environment have led people to expect the unexpected and to fear the ways it might affect their financial future.

Many hope that the dust will begin to settle and things will return to a certain level of normalcy. However, what is important to remember is that the only thing that is certain about the world in which we live is its uncertainty. The world is becoming smaller through the advancements of telecommunications, so much so that it can become confusing and convoluted. The world will only continue to become more complicated and interconnected. This may have the adverse effect of leaving people in a state of information overload and wondering where is the right path for them to become financially secure.

Given this new economic environment, the first step in knowing what to do is to understand the fundamentals of today's economy and how to invest wisely given that context.

As a third-generation financial planner and a professor of finance at W.P. Carey School of Business at Arizona State University, my understanding of financial planning and investing seems to be embedded in my DNA. I was mentored by some of the early pioneers of the financial planning industry: my grandfather and father. At the young age of 10, I began as my father's apprentice, learning about the flow of money, the management of money, and the important psychology that goes with it.

I wrote this book to help you, the reader, understand that managing money and creating wealth isn't rocket science but it does take some insight, tenacity, and skill, which is why many rely on professionals like myself to help them. Unfortunately, with the abundance of financial information aimed at us (some of it is actually incomplete or wrong); most of it becomes noise. Ultimately, some of the noise works: it gets eyeballs on TV screens, clicks on websites, and sales at the newsstands—but, in reality, the deluge of information just confuses and frightens people. I hope to introduce you to a financial mindset that takes into consideration many of the risks and rewards that exist in the 21st century.

This book contains many concepts that can help you take full ownership of your own financial situation. I will show you how to create and stick with a plan so you can grow, protect, and transfer your wealth to future generations.

I don't want to perpetuate misconceptions about investing or financial planning, that is, the delusion that a successful plan can be created overnight through market timing and hot stock tips. Instead, I want to help you to take a step back, looking toward the long term and recognizing what you need, want, and wish for from money. After such a reflection, designing a financial plan that accurately portrays what you want from life, and abiding by that plan long term, can be far easier to accomplish. Throughout the process, you will also learn ways to diversify your portfolio to help protect it from exposure to the forces of the markets.

My overall goal for this book is to positively influence you to take more control over your financial life and move forward financially . . . armed with a new *Money Mindset*.

Who This Book Is For

My intention was to write a book that benefits the general public. People of all ages, income levels, and financial experience can enjoy this quick, easy read. With that being said, the demographics that can benefit the most from *Money Mindset* are Gen-Xers and Millennials, some of whom are students of mine at Arizona State University. They have time on their side to be able to incorporate these concepts and have them work to their advantage.

Our society lacks the proper financial education and urgency to plan and save to be able to utilize money as a tool and focus on long-term financial wellness. Here, I lay out the framework that can help get you started on the right path.

Acknowledgments

Writing a book has many layers with the hope that each layer adds clarification and depth to the project. No layer can be rushed; it takes time to write meaningful and easy-to-read content.

Money Mindset is what it is today because of countless people who committed their time and energy to bring this book into reality. I could not have done it alone. I have great appreciation to all those who contributed to this enormous project. Thank you so very much to everyone who listened to my early vision of *Money Mindset* and believed in the project.

Of all the people in the world, no one has believed in me or supported me more than my high school sweetheart, and now wife, Sara Gold. Her neverending source of joy, love, and happiness is the fountain from which I get strength. Sara has given me countless gifts, but none greater than our three healthy children.

I dedicate this book to my children Kelvin, Savanna, and Bella so they can take the wisdom contained in the book and apply it to their lives. Money does not bring happiness; you must find it within yourselves. Having financial *wisdom*, though, will help provide a financial game plan that can create financial stability so you can focus your attention on aspects of your life that are most important to you. I once heard that all we are to our children are memories. My hope is that your memories of me are filled with love, devotion, and valuable life lessons.

To my parents, Bill and Sharon Gold, thank you for giving me life and for supporting me unconditionally. I often tell people that my mother taught me to love and my father taught me how to work and manage money. Thank you for giving me all the tools I have needed to reach my dreams. I am proud of our heritage and grateful to be your son. I love you both very much.

Life has thrown my family many unexpected challenges, none greater than the loss of my big brother, Kelvin William Gold II. He will forever be remembered in my heart and I will forever look after and love his wife, Jill, and son, Wyatt.

To Jill Gold: Your strength, devotion and love for Wyatt has inspired me to become a better person. I admire everything about you and cherish our relationship. I love you JMOG.

To Wyatt Gold: Words can't express how proud I am of you. Everytime I see you, you remind me more and more of your father. Your father always has and always will be my personal hero. You possess all of his outstanding qualities, and then some. I've enjoyed watching you grow up and can't wait to be a continued part of your life. You can always count on me. I love you buddy.

To Dr. Lisa Gold: Thank you for helping me understand the psychological aspects of decision making and how it can impact one's life. You are the best big sister I could have ever asked for and I will always cherish the memories of our youth, especially "baby bird." I love you.

To Mike Gold, founder of Gold Law Partners, LLP: Thank you for counseling me on the best ways to communicate the importance of estate planning. Taking a complicated topic and breaking it down in an easy-to-follow format is a testament to your knowledge of your field. Thank you also for being my big brother and always looking out for me. Even though we live on opposite ends of the country, I cherish every opportunity to see you. Our moments together always take me back to the wonderful adventures we had as boys. Love you, big bro.

Thanks, love, and gratitude go to my in-laws, John and Sandy Whaley. Thank you for creating and raising your dear daughter, Sara. I never take her for granted and will always devote my life to her happiness.

To my team at Jacob Gold & Associates, Inc., that supports me in providing investment strategies and financial guidance to all of my clients: Thank you to Sherry Kowitz, who has been with me since 2003, for devoting your professional life to my well-being. Your willingness to support the firm in any way needed has helped build the firm to what it is today. To Ida Chaidez, I could not imagine a sweeter person to greet all my clients as they call or visit the office. To Michael Cochell, it's remarkable how similar we are. I have enjoyed working together and enjoy our deep philosophical discussions early in the morning before the rest of the team arrives. Your insights and opinions were carefully crafted into the message of *Money Mindset*. To Dave Scheur, you are a valuable business partner and a wonderful single father. Thank you for believing in me and the vision I have for the firm. Together we will accomplish great things. Your talent for breaking down processes to improve efficiencies has benefited this book and the firm.

To my clients: Thank you for entrusting me to be your financial planner; it is a responsibility that I take very seriously. My hope is that you feel special and cared for every time we communicate. It is an honor getting to know your story and helping you accomplish your financial goals. Please know that my team and I will always put our best foot forward to help you in any way we can.

To Maggie Dietrich at Voya Financial: Several years ago, I was approached to join a team of four independent financial planners who would be later named Voya Retirement Coaches. The team would be the voice of the independent financial planner for the Voya Financial Advisors broker dealer. I am proud to be associated with that team, with you as our leader. Thank you for believing in *Money Mindset* and for helping me find my inner voice. As editor of *Money Mindset*, you have polished my writing and have helped appropriately frame my ideology. Your insights, creativity, loyalty, and devotion are extremely inspiring.

To Sydney LeBlanc, my writing coach and collaborator: Without you this project would have never gotten to paper, it would still be floating around in my head. Thank you for your patience with me as I was figuring out my message. When we first met, I felt that you were a special soul and that we would work well together. Fast-forward to present day, and I am glad that I trusted my intuition: You are everything I hoped and more. Thank you, Syd!

To Doug Coté, Chief Market Strategist at Voya Investment Management: Thank you for agreeing to write such an impactful foreword to *Money Mindset*. I have found your economic forecasts to be accurate and very insightful. Your perspective on tectonic shifts within the energy field was extremely helpful as I was researching the economic impact of North America becoming energy independent. Thank you showing interest in my literary works and wanting to contribute your insights.

To Neal Thompson, President of Thompson Wealth Management, thank you for contributing your energy to this project. Ever since we first met at Horizon High School, I knew you were a person who was going places. You and I both were trained and taught by one of the best in our industry—my father. Keep up the great work, buddy!

To Joe O'Boyle, thank you for taking a personal interest in my book and me. After reading the first three chapters of *Money Mindset*, your comments reshaped the way I looked at the message I was trying to portray. Your keen insights clearly showed me that you live your life by design, not by default. I respect that and look forward to finding ways to work together more in the future.

To Larry Divers of Cannon Financial Institute, you are an inspiration. Your insight and knowledge of the financial industry are woven into *Money Mindset*. Our conversations throughout the years inspired me to relook at some financial concepts that I had taken for granted long ago. You revived me and inspired me to create something that will have lasting impact for future generations.

To Larry Winget, The Pitbull of Personal Development®: Meeting you while appearing in studio for FOX Business was a momentous occasion in my overall career. Since then, you have taken me under your wing to coach and guide me in promoting my brand and literary works. Thank you Larry.

Richard Earle: Back in 2013, as we were diving into our usual philosophical conversations, you planted a seed for the original concept of *Money Mindset*. It was in that moment, you shared with me the notion of looking at money as an energy source. Thank you, my friend, for expanding my universe of thinking.

To Creighton Barker: Thank you for an ever-evolving friendship that I respect and cherish. As boys we played together and thought about our future. Today, we still play but we now talk of our kids' future. You should be proud of the man you are and for the family you are raising. Thank you for letting me be a part of your life and for keeping me out of trouble when we were boys.

Special thanks also go to Paul Barker, Ronnie Metcalf, Brownie Sides, Nancy Sides, Buddy Gore, Larry Rosenthal, Kevin Carter, Avi Kantor, Jim Underhill, Sam Head, Wendy Preston,

Wyatt Gold, Melissa Levin, Patty Barker, Doug Cote, James Nichols, Julie Cooney, Holly Kylen, Marilyn Timbers, Amy Hillman, Tom Bates, Jeanne Elliott, Ashleigh Leite, Marisa Folz, Nancy Mailhot, Teresa Bossone, Mike Egan, Karyn Cavanaugh, Russ Wiles, Rich Linton, Rod Martin, Marty Matyas, Lynne Smith, Tom Hollaran, Mike Berry, Victor Acca, Nancy Bocella, Irene McKenna, Scott Brown, Jon Lara, Cynthia Almanza, Ellen Anderson, Ram Kajal, Adam Hiniker, Tom Habicht, Todd Taylor, Nikki Taylor, Dean Gilderoy, Don Roberts, Eric Kohler, Tina Edwards Christy Hiniker, Melissa Barker, Owen Barker, Mark Reicks, Felicia Chaidez, Jeff Young, Marci Young, Joe Brunsman, Rick Williamson, Trip Metcalf, Pace Barker, Kim Pomeroy Furphy, Glenn Thomas, Wil Everts, Matt Richards, Mark Whaley, Jeff Whaley, Jason Moyes, Sean Graham, Andra Rail, Desmond Barker, Bill Hiniker, Norma Marquez Escarcega, Oscar Escobar Marquez, Chris Tousley, Dave Pagano, Sam Wright, Derek Sroufe, Donna Wright, Octavio Martinez, Ryan Hatch, Greg Horsley, Octavio Marquez, Daniela Marquez, Chad Partington, Scott Pasmore, David Greene, Jeff Rattiner, Julee Grovert, Spencer Metcalf, Dennis Knudsen, Laurel Sroufe, Brett McAvoy, Frank Moskowitz, Luke Kayyem, Ray Boone, Tammy Boone, Richard Shields, Rob Dolman, Patrick Rail, Gary Mizell, Joanne Mizell, Jason Grovert, Kevin Stych, Karl Lindberg, Jill Gold, Dave Wagner, Pete Pallagi, Mckay Ensign, Algis Montiejunas, Nahin Sanchez, Joe Chavez, Joe McDonald, Todd Gatzulis, Richard Earle, Gary Mandel, James Flesner, Luke Sine, Zach Gold, Max Gold, Lily Gold, Brittany Gold, Christina Brunsman, Rob Cope, Tim Tyree, Doug Shaffer, Jacob McDonald, Chase McDonald, Matthew Cope, Rudy Ruybal, Laura Prichard, Scott Holmes, Gary Beier, June Beier, Amy Beier, Charles Beier, Linda Latz, Marty Latz, Tammy Ruybal, Teri McDonald, Christina Brunsman, Jacob Cope, Bryon Allen, Lori Cope, Connor Brunsman, Marc Leach, Voya Financial, Vanguard Group and W.P. Carey School of Business at Arizona State University.

Chapter 1

Money Is Energy

If you think about it, money is an energy source. One of the ways Webster's Dictionary defines energy is "the physical or mental strength that allows you to do things." Money, like gasoline for your vehicle, allows you the ability to do the things you want to do in life. It is literally and figuratively the fuel that propels you through life.

We all need a good amount of energy to fuel our lives—physical energy (sleep, food, and water); mental energy (education, information, conversation); spiritual energy (prayer, meditation, fellowship); energy for our homes, vehicles, and schools (electricity, heating and cooling, gasoline); and economic energy (money and investing).

Everyone has the quest of having enough economic energy to fuel a desired lifestyle without getting into debt, becoming a burden on family or friends, or running out of money. While many have the best of intentions when it comes to managing their money, many ignore those good intentions. Simply put, most people are not planning or saving enough. In fact, Voya Financial research found that only 17 percent of working Americans have a formal financial plan and only 31 percent have a written budget. Simple steps such as these are key foundational building blocks for a secure financial future.[1]

There Is No Silver Bullet

Everybody wants a silver bullet. You know what? I don't blame anyone for this, but guess what: *There isn't one.* Searching for a silver financial bullet is like searching for El Dorado, the mythical "Lost City of Gold." *It just doesn't exist*, so you need to be a realist—a problem-solving realist—who understands the situation, creates a realistic plan, and follows it. Unfortunately, when people get desperate, they place even more hope in finding a silver bullet to bail them out. Many times, they end up hurting themselves by jumping from one quick fix to another.

Forget the magic bullet/quick fix solution. When you were little, you had to crawl before you could walk and walk before you could run. If you tried to do it in any other sequence you would probably fall and get hurt. It's the same with money, especially in the current environment, in which things are rapidly changing. If you get ahead of yourself, you will feel as though you have little control. Without the proper *money mindset*, you may feel that you are not in control *at all*. When we are not in control of something, we fear it, and the mind tends to dwell on the worst-case scenario. People make mistakes when they are fearful, and run the risk of taking on too much risk.

There is a strategy in understanding money. You must be defensive and try to either avoid or minimize the pitfalls and risks. The goal is to stay within an area where you are comfortable. Allow your money—over time—to compound and grow without getting distracted by the noise coming at you from all sides. This noise can paralyze people when they don't have the necessary knowledge or tools to help them analyze and understand what is going on and how it may affect them in the long term.

T. Boone Pickens wisely said, "The older I get, the more I see a straight path where I want to go. If you're going to hunt elephants, don't get off the trail for a rabbit."

Building Your "Financial Foundation"

The path to financial prosperity is not easy. You need to understand your time horizon as well as your risk tolerance before you can even begin investing. When you invest in financial knowledge, take control of your assets based on what you know, and heed the advice of skilled financial professionals, you can increase your chances of financial success. You will not be simply rolling the dice, hoping that things will go your way.

The first step in building a financial game plan is similar to the process of building a house—start with a solid base: a financial foundation. Throughout the rest of *Money Mindset* I will explain all of the pieces that you should incorporate into your foundation, along with the process to follow your plan. But for now, let me quickly lay out some of the basics of a financial foundation.

To begin, be sure to pay your (future) self first. What does that mean? It means that—along with paying your monthly bills and other expenses—you will set aside a portion of your income for long-term savings. I encourage you to attempt to save 10 to 15 percent of your gross pay, working up to that goal over time if needed. Put that money into your 401(k), IRA, brokerage account, or your savings account. This becomes a positive habit and has the potential to help build wealth. Trust me; you will learn to live without the money in your hands each month.

Regardless of net worth, have at least basic estate planning documents, such as a last will and testament, a medical power of attorney, and a durable power of attorney. Having proper insurance coverage is an important part of your foundation, too. It should help cover your liabilities if you were to pass away prematurely, become ill, or get into an accident.

If you are saving for retirement, have no credit card debt, and have established basic estate planning documents, general insurance protection, and about three to six months of cash in an emergency fund, you are building a strong financial foundation.

Unfortunately, many times people will skip the foundation of the process, and they will think, "Well economically speaking, things are going well. I want to invest now, maybe buy some stocks, and then as that money grows, I'll pay off some of my debt. It's no big deal." However, you are opening Pandora's box, because you already have the liability, and yet now that you have the resources, instead of paying down your debt (e.g., credit cards), you have put the money into investments with components of risk that you can't control. It may be that you will wind up having that same debt, and that the cash you put into stocks that you could have used to pay down your debt is now worth less due to an unexpected decline in the capital markets. Don't put the cart before the horse.

Instead, align yourself to be more like the tortoise in the fable of the tortoise and the hare. We need to be moving slowly with a methodical strategy, with the least amount of emotion, and with as much time and as much diversification as possible.

What's Ahead?

In the next chapter, you will learn how the ways you think about money can affect you positively or negatively.

KEY INSIGHTS FROM THIS CHAPTER

- Money can be thought of as an energy source to help propel you through life.
- Move forward financially with a clear focus and strategy, using time and portfolio diversification to your advantage.
- You will be more clear and confident in your strategy if you have a strong foundation.
- Before you pay your monthly bills and other expenses, set aside a portion of your income to save, for example, 10 to 15 percent of your gross income.

Note

1. Voya Retire Ready Index™, Voya Financial, http://corporate.voya .com/newsroom/media-kits/voya-retire-ready-index.

Chapter 2

The Psychology
of Money

In this chapter, you will learn how the ways we think about money can affect us positively or negatively.

Many of our attitudes about money are formed in childhood. These attitudes affect our behavior and actions throughout our lives, and even affect the outcome of our financial future. Many people discount or underestimate the power of our money attitudes in our decision-making and planning.

We have beliefs and attitudes about everything that is important to us in life. For example, we have attitudes about politics, religion, war, marriage, and, of course, about money. How can you have an *attitude* about money? Well, your attitude is what money means to you. How do you feel about money? How much does money influence all of your decisions in life (not just your financial ones)?

Simply, your money attitude is your way of thinking about money. And it can affect you negatively or positively.

Glenn D. Wilson, one of Britain's best-known psychologists, once said, "Money evokes conditioned emotional responses.

People become obsessive about money—it gives them a buzz like an addiction. It has commonalities with food, which might suggest an evolutionary origin for our craving. And money is more than just a means to an end. It prompts behavior that cannot be explained by its utilitarian value. People rolling in money still seek more of it, as though they can never get enough. They will sacrifice other values such as family and friends in favor of accumulating money. They chase money for the sake of money or perhaps to keep ahead of the Joneses."[1]

Money is such an important part of our lives because it affects our relationships, our career choices, our education, our families, our retirement, our charitable giving, and much more. How do *you* feel about money, and when you think about money what thoughts come to mind? What thoughts do you have from childhood about how money affected your home life? Did your parents argue about money? Did you feel worried about money? Fast-forward to now. Do you argue with your spouse or children about money? These are important questions to ask yourself to uncover your attitudes toward money.

For me, money attitudes were embedded in me as a young child. I can recall countless lessons that I learned while sitting at the kitchen table. My older brother Mike and I were often pretend audience members in our living room, as my father practiced his various financial presentations. Today, I'm trying to embed that same financial education and *money mindset* into my three children.

Your past experiences are the biggest influence on your attitude and feelings about money. Many psychologists believe your attitude is a learned behavior and that what is learned can also be unlearned. Since our psychology influences and shapes our financial situations, it's time to get at those underlying emotional reasons that may be holding you back. Many of us get emotional about money rather than dealing with it in a realistic, unemotional manner. And we also have huge fears about money, especially when we are in the throes of managing it and investing in the stock market.

With a healthier attitude towards money, we can continue on our path to financial success and retirement readiness. Patience, persistence, and an end goal, or "vision," will help us on our journey.

The Science of Fear and Greed

Let's look at some of the ways emotions are processed in the brain and how those emotions can interfere with clear decision-making. We call these "cognitive and emotional biases."

Daniel Kahneman, recipient of the Nobel Prize in Economic Sciences for his seminal work in psychology, is considered by many to be the Godfather of neuroeconomics and behavioral finance. Kahneman and collaborator Amos Tversky, a Stanford mathematical psychologist, developed many theories which identify and explain irrational human economic choices.

Cognitive Biases

Cognitive biases are tendencies in thinking that influence how we make decisions. The mind acts on perception, not reality. As a result, we tend to think the current situation will continue forever. Cognitive biases can cause us to make inaccurate judgments, decisions, and interpretations. Although it's impossible to completely avoid cognitive biases, it *is* possible to understand what they are so that we can look for them when they arise and adjust our judgments as needed.

People fear a future without enough money, and what that would do to them and their family. Surprisingly, this fear can, at times, hinder someone from reaching financial goals.

Fear Bias

Example #1: Loss Aversion In 1979, Kahneman and Tversky finalized their theory of Loss Aversion. They confirmed that, where money is concerned, *we prefer avoiding losses to making gains*. Put another way, the pain of losing things is usually greater than the pleasure of acquiring them. In fact, their theory concluded that investment losses have more than twice the impact of investment gains on people's minds.

Example #2: Confirmation Bias This is the explanation for why people tend to search for information that authenticates their own opinions, but pay no attention to information that invalidates their beliefs. For example, some people who identify most closely with conservative politics may prefer watching Fox News rather than a more liberal channel such as MSNBC. The reason for this is that each network will often confirm their viewers' political and social point of view. Confirmation bias creates a one-sided view and can cause serious problems when investing. For example, have you noticed that as soon as you invest in a fund or buy a stock, you start looking for reasons why your decision was right? Once a fund or stock is bought, we tend to look for information that confirms the investment is a good one while ignoring information that the investment may be bad or questionable.

Greed biases, listed in the next section, are similar to fear biases in that they are rooted in specific neurological functions; the greed is not simply a hunger for money.

Greed Bias

Example #1: The House-Money Effect This common bias is based on the premise that people are more willing to take risks with money they obtained easily or unexpectedly. For example, investors might take more risks with money they inherited or won while gambling on vacation in Las Vegas than the money they set aside from their paychecks. It is a tendency to feel like gains are "free money." It's what poker players call "house money." People then abandon their traditional risk management techniques, resulting in greater risk than that with which they would otherwise feel comfortable.

Example #2: Self-Attribution Self-attribution is the tendency for people to take credit for successful investment outcomes while blaming unsuccessful outcomes on bad luck or on external directives that they could not know or control. For example, perhaps you were fortunate enough to be one of the first private investors in Starbucks before it went public. You might say, "Look how smart I am!" However, the opposite might have happened if you were unlucky enough to have invested in Enron. You would have "excused" your subsequent losses by saying, "No one could have predicted that."

Solutions and Help

Now that I've described a few investor behaviors and money attitudes, you might begin to recognize such behaviors in yourself as well as the attitudes you have that are holding *you* back from realizing your goals. The secret is to take control of your money by taking control of your mind. And the best way to overcome the psychological biases is to be familiar with them, be self-aware when you are feeling extreme emotions, and to have a methodical financial plan. To have a methodical plan, you have to "Start with *why*," a principle of success explained in Simon Sinek's book about why companies and people fail and/or succeed. You must "believe" in what you do and you must first know *why* you are doing it. We need to reflect on our beliefs and the reasons why we are going through the motions of financial or retirement planning.

What's Ahead?

In the next chapter we will talk about how retirement may look in the 21st century, how it has changed, and why it will be different from our parents' retirement. Pension plans are changing, the underfunding of Social Security is looming, people are living longer, and managing money today is much different than it was 30 years ago. We need to understand the reasons behind these and other changes and challenges in order to understand the *why*.

KEY INSIGHTS FROM THIS CHAPTER

- Many of us get emotional about money, which can lead to poor decision making.
- To take control of your money, take control of your mind.
- Reflect on your beliefs and the reasons *why* you are going through the motions of financial or retirement planning.
- Greed biases and fear biases are rooted in specific neurological functions, so be aware of these biases in yourself.
- Be self-aware when you are feeling extreme emotions, and have a methodical financial plan.

Note

1. Glenn D. Wilson, "The Psychology of Money," www.gresham.ac.uk/lectures-and-events/the-psychology-of-money.

Chapter 3

New Retirement Paradigm

In this chapter we look at how retirement has changed, and why it will be different from our parents' and grandparents' retirements.

Throughout this book, I emphasize that money is energy and that we all have our own psychology about money. You have learned what elements contribute to your attitudes about money as well as how your financial behavior is impacted. Most of us realize that we will have various financial challenges as we approach retirement. We need to think about how to design a plan that supports each individual—a plan that evolves as our needs and desires change.

Perhaps Eric Hoffer, an American philosopher who was awarded the Presidential Medal of Freedom in February 1983, said it best: "In a time of drastic change, it is the learners who inherit the future. The learned find themselves equipped to live in a world that no longer exists."

The Coming Crisis in Retirement Planning

We are entering a new paradigm. The retirement of our parents is no longer the reality of what our own retirement will look like. And the rules of the game from prior decades are no longer relevant. According to Robert C. Merton, a Nobel Prize–Winner in Economic Sciences, there is a coming crisis in retirement planning. Merton says, "Our approach to saving is all wrong: We need to think about monthly income, not net worth."[1]

Merton is correct in stating that the traditional approach to saving is misguided. The challenge—and the goal—is to design a custom savings plan that will help us generate enough annual cash flow—or income—to cover our expenses. The total cash flow needs to be an aggregation of Social Security benefits, possible pension income and personal savings and broken down into monthly income to become a stronger planning tool for us.

So, if we are trying to abide by the old rules, some of us might fall short of our retirement goals. We need to realistically look at money the way it should be looked at in this 21st century—not through the lens of the past, but using the most effective strategies of today.

The question should not be at what age do you want to retire, but at what income.

Why Is Retirement So Different Today?

While there are many reasons that retirement looks very different today than it once did, I want to focus on three reasons: (1) life expectancy, (2) disappearing pensions, and (3) the uncertain future of Social Security.

Life Expectancy

This realization should come as no surprise: Due to advances in medical care and better diets and exercise, we are living longer. In 1970, we could be expected to live to be about 74 years old. In contrast, in 2012, life expectancy was up to nearly 80 years old.[2] While six years doesn't seem like a long time, it means that the money we were setting aside for our retirement has to last six more years. If we think we can live on $5,000 per month in retirement, then that means we have to save an additional $360,000 in order to avoid having our money run out.

Disappearing Pensions

Once a primary underpinning of a comfortable retirement, pensions are fading away at a rapid pace. A pension provides a regular payment during a person's retirement; the payment comes from an investment fund to which that person or their employer contributed during their working life.

The dynamics of pensions are very powerful. When an employee has a pension at a corporation, the corporation is using its own money to fund, in essence, an income stream that the employee can't outlive. What is so remarkable about that is not only is the company providing the actual dollar amount in the form of a contribution to a big pot, but the corporation is also responsible for the management of those dollars. They own the risk. You'll get a monthly income stream that you can't outlive. The size of your payout is simply a function of a basic formula that factors in how long you worked, how much you earned and your life expectancy.

A pension becomes a very expensive plan for a corporation to provide their employees. Not only is it more costly to invest more in the pension because people are living longer but also because the markets are much more volatile than they have been in prior decades. The percentage of workers in the private sector whose only retirement account is a defined benefit pension plan is now 10 percent, down from 60 percent in the early 1980s.[3]

The 401(k), which is named after a section of the Internal Revenue Code, was developed by accident in the Revenue Act of 1978. The goal of the Revenue Act of 1978 was to limit corporate executives' access to the perks of cash-deferred retirement plans. In 1980, thanks to the pioneering work of Ted Benna, a benefits consultant who created the first employer-based retirement savings program 30 years ago, companies began interpreting the law to create 401(k) plans that would allow full-time employees to fund their retirement with pretax dollars, often with employers making matching contributions. By 1984, the 401(k) had become the primary retirement vehicle for Americans.

With a 401(k), you are using your own money and are responsible for choosing how to allocate. Put simply, in a 401(k), "you own the risk." If you don't manage it appropriately, it might not last you through retirement. Given the shift from pensions to 401(k)s, it's increasingly incumbent upon the individual to take control of their retirement planning.

The Uncertain Future of Social Security

A third factor leading to the shift in the retirement landscape is Social Security.

First, let's talk a bit about Social Security.

The Social Security Act of 1935 was drafted during President Franklin D. Roosevelt's first term and was passed by Congress as part of the New Deal. At the time, the average life expectancy was 62 and, in order to begin collecting Social Security, you had to be 65. This essentially meant that most people were not expected to live to collect money from the system into which they had paid. In addition, in 1935, for every person collecting Social Security benefits, there were 40 people paying into the system. For much of its history, Social Security was strictly a pay-as-you-go system, with current tax receipts funding current benefits.

In 1983, under President Ronald Reagan, Congress decided to raise the payroll taxes to build up a reserve for the coming onslaught of baby-boomer retirees. The increased payroll taxes were then invested in special nontradable Treasury bonds, with interest credited to the system. Another way of saying this is that the U.S. Government began to legally use the Social Security reserve dollars to fund its own spending. Today, the Social Security reserve system is full of government IOUs—special nontraded Treasury bonds. As interest rates eventually begin to rise, the cost to service those IOUs will go up, creating more of a financial obligation for the U.S. government.

The System Is Running Out of Energy

Social Security trustees project that the reserves for the retirement and disability trust funds could tap out by 2033, due to the increased number of baby boomers becoming eligible for benefits and the longer life expectancies of those who are collecting benefits. Absent a bailout from general revenues, insolvency could result in across-the-board Social Security benefit cuts of about 23 percent. The average 70-year-old today is probably not expecting to see the day that Social Security becomes insolvent. But if actual insolvency comes sooner, rather than by 2033, that is just what may happen.[4] The fact is that it will need to be addressed at some point, but is not likely to be resolved soon.

Let's be clear about the future of Social Security: there is a crisis looming. The ratio of working people to retired people in America is only increasing; as of 2010, there were only 2.9 people contributing to the Social Security pot for every 1 person collecting. Comparing this to the 40:1 ratio that existed in 1935 when Social Security was created.

At some point, Congress will have to address these issues and make some difficult adjustments. Unfortunately, the decision to make the needed adjustments to Social Security is something no politician wants to face. One of the most important goals of politicians is to get re-elected and the largest segment of registered voters tends to be those currently receiving Social Security.[5] Therefore, politicians will most likely kick the can down the road for as long as they can afford to do so.

In 2013, the cochairs of President Obama's Fiscal Responsibility Commission, Alan Simpson and Erskine Bowles, recommended three main changes to Social Security. The suggestions were to (1) increase the taxable maximum on income to 90 percent of all income. This solution was projected to raise $238 billion over the next decade. (2) Recommend a different measure of inflation to slow cost-of-living adjustments. (3) Raise the retirement age to 68 in 2050 and 69 in 2075. In the short term, it means that people who were "banking" on collecting benefits at 65 might have to work longer. But by pushing out the retirement age, there may not be a cap on the wages that people pay into Social Security. At some point, we should recognize that these three changes will come to light in some shape or form, and the tax rates may need to go up to fund that as well.

Did you know that 24 percent of the federal budget, or $823 billion, was paid out for Social Security? This amount provided monthly retirement benefits averaging $1,294 to 37.9 million retired workers as of December 2013. Social Security also provided benefits to 2.9 million spouses and children of retired workers, 6.2 million surviving children and spouses of deceased workers, and 11 million disabled workers and their eligible dependents during the same time period.[6]

People will need more personal assets to make up for the lack of pension income and possibly reduced Social Security benefits. People have more financial challenges than ever before. They have less pension income, are living longer, and are concerned about the insolvency issues with Social Security being underfunded.

What's Ahead?

In future chapters, we'll discuss how you can appropriately plan and make up for that deficit. From vision to execution, we explore what it will take for you to become financially independent.

Let's also keep in mind what Merton said about our approach to saving. He is right—ever since pensions have been replaced by 401(k)s the conversation about retirement has shifted to account values. The conversation should still be about income replacement, and how much income can be generated by the dollar amount invested.

KEY INSIGHTS FROM THIS CHAPTER

- We are in the midst of a new retirement paradigm. Our retirements will not look like our parents' retirements.
- There are three main reasons why retirement looks different today: (1) longer life expectancy, (2) disappearing pensions, and (3) the uncertain future of Social Security.
- People will need more personal assets to make up for the lack of pension income and possibly reduced Social Security benefits.

Notes

1. Robert C. Merton, "The Crisis in Retirement Planning," *Harvard Business Review*, July–August 2014.
2. Bahar Gholipour, "U.S. Life Expectancy Continues to Climb," *Washington Post*, December 8, 2014, www.washingtonpost.com /national/health-science/US-life-expectancy-continues-to-climb /2014/12/05/9edb2ffe-4fc2-11e4-8c24-487e92bc997b_story.html.
3. "Just How Common Are Defined Benefit Plans?" CNN Money, http://money.cnn.com/retirement/guide/pensions_basics.moneymag /index7.htm?iid=EL.
4. Rachel Greszler, "History Suggests That Social Security Insolvency Is Coming Sooner Than Expected," The Heritage Foundation, www .heritage.org/research/reports/2013/06/history-suggests-social-security-insolvency-is-coming-sooner-than-projected.
5. "How Should the Government Change Social Security?" *Wall Street Journal*, August 13, 2014, http://online.wsj.com/articles/how-should-the-government-change-social-security-1407931198.
6. Bernie Becker, "Medicare, Social Security March toward Insolvency," The Hill, http://thehill.com/policy/healthcare/213491-medicare-social-security-head-toward-insolvency-at-slower-rate.

Chapter 4

The "Why" of Financial Management

In this chapter we explore what it will take for you to become financially independent. But first, I need to stress how important it is to have a respect for the emotional, as well as the economic, aspects of wealth. Both play a critical role in your financial independence.

In order to address the emotional aspects of your personal financial management, you must start with the "why" of your ultimate goal. What does that mean? Simply, you need to understand your life's dreams and why they are important to you. What are you working toward? Why are you investing? What is your end game? And do you have a process to achieve your life's dreams? Fortunately, if you start with the "why" the rest will follow. The rest primarily includes the "what" and the "how" of getting there.

What's Your "Why"?

The first step in discovering your "why" is to recognize what makes you tick. For example, my wife and three kids are what make me tick. The love and support I receive from them, and the fulfilling feeling that I receive by reciprocating, is my "everything." My "why" is to provide a consistently healthy and safe ecosystem for my family.

If you are married or in a long-term relationship, you might want to have a conversation with your partner about the "why." Where do the two of you want to be in 10 years, or 20 years? Do you want to have a beautiful retirement to spend more time with the grandkids, do you want to sail around the world, do you want to devote more time to volunteering at charities and to help those in need? What is your end game, and do you both agree?

Starting with the "why" is the beginning of everything. It's what motivates you to achieve your financial goals. Most people already have at least a general idea of how they want to live the rest of their lives. Unfortunately, many may get so caught up in their everyday lives that they lose sight of the big picture.

The goal then is to get to a point where money can help you achieve your ideal life vision. Money is essentially a conduit to get you to support your "why." Once there, you are in control and can stand on your own two feet with grace and pride.

When I ask my clients about their "why," some will quickly respond by saying, "I want to have $1 million, or $5 million, or I want to have a jet plane." Many will jump ahead to the conclusion before figuring out what they truly want out of life and what it will take to get them there financially. Maybe they don't need $1 million, or maybe $1 million is not enough. Basing your end goal on assumptions can distract you from honing in on what you *actually need*. Ask yourself: What are your needs, wants, and wishes, both now and for the future?

A client of mine, Jim Flesner, once shared with me something I will never forget: "There are three things we all need in order to be happy—someone to love, something to do, and something to look forward to."

Once you realize there are no shortcuts and you understand the essence of your goal, then you track it and plan accordingly. On your path, you'll need to silence all that noise from the media, markets, friends, and even the loud (often biased!) voices in your head. This allows you to direct your time, energy, and thoughts elsewhere, knowing that you went through the right process to stay focused on your "why."

Not Planning Is the Same as Planning to Fail: Where to Start

Do you have a written financial plan or process you follow to achieve your goals? Benjamin Franklin said, "If you fail to plan, you are planning to fail."

When it comes to your finances you may know you want financial independence, but not know how to get there. Individuals should begin by analyzing their current and needed monthly cash flow, breaking down the fixed and variable components. This is the beginning step in creating a formal budget that can establish parameters around your spending.

Everybody has a "magic number" that represents their desired lifestyle. The difficulty lies in calculating the number correctly and then sticking to it. This holds true during your working years and in retirement.

Don't forget. Make sure when you are designing your plan that you don't miss something. You don't want to realize 5, 10, 15, or 20 years down the road that you miscalculated and you have underfunded your lifestyle or retirement. There are *no* do-overs.

You can always kick the tires with software. Online programs like myOrangeMoney™ by Voya Financial (http://voya.com/tool/orange-money#step1) can assist you in finding your "magic number" for retirement. Software programs are a good start to help quantify how much is enough, what type of return on your investments is required, how much you need to contribute per year, and for how many years your money will need to compound in order to reach your goal. Each software system will have different variables, so it is always good to run a few scenarios on a couple of programs and then review it with a professional who can validate its assumptions.

Former NFL coach Herman Edwards says, "A goal without a plan is just a wish."

Just remember, the moment you pull certain triggers, there may be no going back. For instance, if you're out of corporate America for a couple of years, you may not be able to get the same quality of job if you want to go back. You may experience age discrimination, and jobs with your particular set of skills may be harder to come by. Today, there's more of a burden on all of us to work harder and think smarter.

Be Prepared for the Thunderstorms

I believe it is important to have a conservative and realistic plan, because when times get tough, emotions can run high. People feel vulnerable because of their own mental biases, and an investor can feel himself or herself "going off the rails." These are the moments when it is critical to stay true to your plan. The only way someone can firmly believe in a plan and have hope in that plan, is if they err on the side of caution. Try to always plan for the worst and hope for the best.

It is important to be prepared, too. As a teenager, I was fortunate enough to achieve the rank of Eagle Scout and now my son is working toward that same goal. We both understand and believe in the Boy Scout motto: "Be Prepared." If you are out in the wilderness and it starts raining and you don't have rain gear, you are exposed to nature's forces. By that time, it's too late; you are soaked. Once soaked, if you can't get warm and dry by nightfall, the situation could become fatal.

We recognize that, in life, there are going to be a lot of thunderstorms. There will be many events that we didn't anticipate or even imagine. Whenever you're put in a difficult situation, if you haven't had a moment to think about what you could do in that situation, you may very well end up making an emotional decision. That emotional decision may end up impeding you from getting to where you really want to go, financially or otherwise.

Often, we fear the things we don't know, or the landmines we can't see. We're all vulnerable, but even more so if we don't have that plan. Without a plan, if the markets decline, you might say to yourself, "I've got to get out. I'm already behind the eight-ball. I don't have enough money for retirement and what I'm going to lose will delay my retirement; I've got to get out." So you get out, and you feel relieved of your fear because that's what you're truly looking for—freedom from that fear. Then you don't know when to get back into the market.

There are times when we may find ourselves losing focus. It is during these times that you may need a sounding board to let you know if everything in your plan is okay or if adjustments are in order.

The wisdom and experience of navigating a plan may be the most important value proposition that financial planners have in the 21st century. A big part of the responsibility of the financial planner is to advise you on how the world affects your plan, how to avoid making big financial mistakes, and how to plan for your future retirement readiness. A financial planner can help design a plan and be your financial coach. He or she can be your sounding board and assure you that you have someone who understands you and the markets.

What's Ahead?

In the next chapter, we'll discuss the power of compound interest and the erosive effect of inflation.

KEY INSIGHTS FROM THIS CHAPTER

- It is important to have a respect for the emotional, as well as the economic, aspects of wealth, as both will play a critical role in your financial independence.
- Start with the "why"—this is the beginning of everything good.
- Silence all the distractions and stick to your plan.
- Make sure you are designing your plan based on numbers. Use myOrangeMoney™ by Voya Financial (http://voya.com/tool/orange-money#step1) to find your "magic number" for monthly income in retirement.
- A financial advisor can help design a plan and be your financial coach. He or she can be our sounding board and let you know that you have someone who understands you and the markets.

Chapter 5

The Power of Compound Interest and the Erosive Effect of Inflation

S o far in *Money Mindset* I have stressed the importance of having a plan to accomplish your financial goals. After you determine your goals and construct your plan, the wealth management process begins to unfold. There is a lot to learn and digest about the process, and in upcoming chapters I will break down for you the impact of taxes and asset allocation, how to evaluate your risk tolerance and build an investment portfolio, and finally, how to monitor your portfolio and rebalance it when needed.

But first, this chapter discusses the power of compound interest and the erosive effect of inflation. Remember, you need to have the right financial mindset in order to meet your goals and have your investments live up to their full potential.

The Power of Compound Interest

Albert Einstein, a Noble Prize Laureate in physics who studied the biggest mysteries of our universe, said, "Compound interest is the eighth wonder of the world. He who understands it, earns it . . . he who doesn't . . . pays it."

Let's explore the power of compounding by learning the mathematical Rule of 72.

The Rule of 72 is a simplified way to estimate how long an investment will take to double, given a fixed annual rate of interest. By dividing 72 by the annual rate of return, you can get a rough estimate of how many years it will take for the initial investment to duplicate itself. For example, the rule of 72 states that if a $100,000 grew by an annual return of 10 percent per year, it would take approximately 7.2 years [(72/10) = 7.2] to turn into $200,000.

Rule of 72

Rate of Return	Approx. # of Years for Money to Double
2%	36 years
3%	24 years
5%	14.4 years
7%	10.3 years
9%	8 years
10%	7.2 years
12%	6 years

Now, let me share with you a story about when I first learned and understood the power of compound interest. I was in Dr. Fawley's sixth-grade math class. One day in class, Dr. Fawley asked us if we liked money. *Of course*, we responded, and just like that he had our undivided attention. He then went on to say that he wanted to give each student a choice between two imaginary options. Would you rather receive (a) $1,000 per day for 30 days ($30,000 over the 30 days) or (b) a penny the first day, two pennies the next day, four pennies the following day, and so on, with the amount doubling every day for 30 days in all?

He gave us a few seconds to decide which of the two options we would choose. He then asked everyone who wanted the $30,000 of free imaginary money to raise their hand; most hands went up, including mine. Then he asked who wanted the penny compounded daily for 30 days. Few students raised their hands. My guess, now looking back, was that those students who chose option (b) must have known there was a trick involved.

Those few students who thought it was a trick question were right; compound interest is one of the best-known tools for growing wealth. By day 22, assuming the value to double daily, the compounded amount would have been $20,971.52. By day 30, it would be valued at $5,368,709.12.

Day 1: $.01	Day 6: $.32	Day 11: $10.24	Day 16: $327.68	Day 21: $10,485.76	Day 26: $335,544.32
Day 2: $.02	Day 7: $.64	Day 12: $20.48	Day 17: $655.36	Day 22: $20,971.52	Day 27: $671,088.64
Day 3: $.04	Day 8: $1.28	Day 13: $40.96	Day 18: $1,310.72	Day 23: $41,943.04	Day 28: $1,342,177.28
Day 4: $.08	Day 9: $2.56	Day 14: $81.92	Day 19: $2,621.44	Day 24: $83,886.08	Day 29: $2,684,354.56
Day 5: $.16	Day 10: $5.12	Day 15: $163.84	Day 20: $5,242.88	Day 25: $167,772.16	Day 30: $5,368,709.12

Compound interest is often called the eighth wonder of the world (as Einstein said) because it seems to possess magical powers. Compound interest can help us to achieve our financial goals, such as becoming a millionaire, retiring comfortably, or being financially independent. Yet, this is easier said than done. . . .

Make Time Work for You

Many people don't recognize the power of how their money can grow if invested over the long term. The challenge is making sure dollars are truly allocated appropriately and that some portions of your savings are kept liquid for life's unanticipated emergencies. That's why it's important to be a disciplined and consistent saver with a plan for how your investments are allocated.

I always tell people that there's never a "right" time to invest. When the markets are down, people don't want to invest because they're afraid of losing money. That's human nature. They think, "Oh, I'll just wait until we hit bottom and then I'll start investing." The problem with that thinking is no one knows when the bottom will occur or how to detect it. If the markets are up, people are nervous about investing because they're afraid of buying high and experiencing a crash with their money. If you're waiting for the ideal time to start investing, you will be waiting indefinitely because there will always be ups and downs, always reasons why you may not want to invest or why you want to spend those dollars on other things. There's never a perfect time to invest, but the sooner you start investing and begin a habit of saving, the money you accumulate can grow substanitally over the years.

The Cost of Procrastination

Let's say you have a goal to accumulate $1 million dollars by the time you turn 65. Assuming that you are 25 years old right now, how much do you think you would need to start saving per month to reach your goal? Mathematically speaking, you would need to begin saving approximately $353 per month, earning a 7.27 percent rate of return per year, for 40 years, in order to amass $1,000,000.

As a side note, over a 20-year time period, ending December 31, 2012, the S&P 500 index, "the U.S. stock market," earned an 8.21 percent rate of return per year, while an investment in the Barclay's Aggregate Bond Index, "the U.S. bond market," earned 6.34 percent. A weighted portfolio of 50 percent stocks (S&P 500 Index), and 50 percent bonds (Barclay's Aggregate Bond Index) resulted in a blended return of 7.27 percent per year over those 20 years.

As I mentioned, it's never the perfect time to invest. People live their lives, have their families, send their kids to school and they think, "Oh, once the kids are out on their own, that's really when we'll start investing for our retirement."

Well, the problem with waiting is that the longer you wait, the more you have to save per month because you have less time for your money to earn at a compounded rate.

What if you are 55 years old right now and are just beginning to save for retirement? How much do you think you would need to start saving per month to reach the goal of $1,000,000 by the time you turn 65? You would need to begin saving approximately $5,692 per month, earning a 7.27 percent rate of return per year, for 10 years in order to amass $1,000,000.

This amount, $5,692, is a lot of money to save each month, and is more than most households' total monthly income.

Time begins to work against you the longer you delay saving for retirement. The chart below demonstrates the differences.

Monthly Investment

Age 25	Age 35	Age 45	Age 55
$353	$777	1,857	$5,692

The chart is based on the premise of a 7.27 percent rate of return, solving for a future value of $1,000,000 and present value of $0, for the number of years remaining before the age of 65.

The Story of Larry and Earl

Let me tell you the story of Larry and Earl, two college roommates of the same age. While in college, they both enjoyed dreaming about their future. To help make their dreams become a reality, they determined they each would need to start saving a portion of their income upon graduation. Larry and Earl made a commitment to each other to save at least $4,000 per year until age 65.

After graduation, they both went their separate ways, building their careers, and eventually they lost touch with each other. Time quickly passed and before they knew it, it was time for their 20th college reunion. They were excited to see each other after so many years, and were eager to catch up. Larry shared with Earl the ups and downs of his life and why he was not able to live up to their shared commitment to save $4,000 each year like he had hoped. Larry confessed that for the first 10 years after college he had focused on everything *except* saving. However, he was proud to announce to Earl that he began saving $4,000 a year for the past 10 years.

After hearing Larry's story, Earl then shared how he diligently saved, prioritizing it above spending his money frivolously. He explained how he did this. He told him that saving money quickly became a positive habit and he didn't miss the money that he had been saving. The process of saving and seeing that balance grow in his account became a rewarding experience. Both Larry and Earl were now savers. But, "Late Larry" missed out on years of compounding, while "Early Earl" had the benefit of his money compounding for a much longer period of time.

Fast-forward another 20 years, while both Larry and Earl stayed true to their renewed commitment to save at least $4,000 per year. Forty years after their original promise to each other, their investments had grown to impressive amounts. Larry had invested $120,000 over a 30-year time period that earned him a 7.27 percent rate of return. His nest egg had grown to $431,599.35. Earl, on the other hand, invested $160,000 over a 40-year time period that earned him a 7.27 percent rate of return.

How much more money does "Early Earl" have than "Late Larry"?

"Early Earl" saved $40,000 more than "Late Larry," but did that make much of a difference? Absolutely it did. Earl's $160,000 grew to $949,879. By investing a decade earlier, Earl's savings were twice as large as Larry's.

$4,000 per Year, 7.27% Return

Age	Larry	Earl
25–34	$0	$4,000
35–64	$4,000	$4,000
Amount Invested	$120,000	$160,000
Value at 65	$431,599.35	$949,879.31

This story should help send the message that it is essential to start planning for your future and saving as early as possible. You can't just sit back and think, "Oh, I've got plenty of time, I'll think about that later, I've got a lot of years ahead of me." However, those years go by fast. For Millennials and Gen X-ers, your most valuable financial asset is time. You may not have a lot in net worth or income, but you have the time to invest and save. You're going to be much better off 20 or 30 years from now than you would be if you focus on the YOLO (you only live once) mindset.

Henry David Thoreau said, "Wealth is the ability to fully experience life."

The Erosive Effects of Inflation

My father explained to me at a young age that inflation occurs when we have too many dollars chasing too few goods. As the purchasing price of the dollar declines, it takes more to buy less. For example, during World War I, Germany created an enormous amount of debt by issuing bonds and was freely rolling out more German marks via the printing press. Germany was planning to have its surrendered enemies pay the debt after their victory. As we all know, the opposite happened. After Germany surrendered, they were forced to sign the Treaty of Versailles. The Treaty meant that Germany had to pay reparations to the allies and large swaths of its territory were divided, which created hyperinflation in Germany. In October 1923, German prices rose at a rate of 41 percent per day. By November 1923, one dollar equaled one trillion marks. This resulted in people using wheelbarrows full of marks to buy a single loaf of bread.[1] This all happened because the German government spent more money than they were bringing in, and eventually, devalued its currency so much that it became nearly worthless.

Looking at Inflation Today

It is important to remember that while you are working, your income usually goes up with the cost of living, and you won't exponentially feel the pain of inflation. That will change when you are retired and living on a fixed income; inflation will erode the purchasing power of your money. It is helpful to adjust your income every year to keep up with inflation, which means that you have to be taking out more and more every year. Inflation has been very volatile over the past 30 years. Yet, people should anticipate at least 2 to 3 percent inflation every year, and some years it could be a lot more than that.

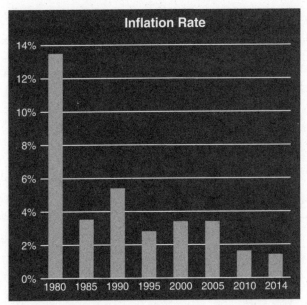

SOURCE: www.usinflationcalculator.com/inflation/historical-inflation-rates/.

The Shrinking Dollar

If you were to use a 3 percent inflation rate, how much do you think inflation would negatively affect your purchasing power over 20 years?

If you need $100,000 a year today to cover all your fixed and variable expenses, in 20 years you will need $180,000 to maintain the same standard of living. The other way to look at it is that $100,000 a year, 20 years from now, will be worth only $55,367 in today's dollars.

You need to save enough to draw an income to cover your current expenses, but you've got to put enough away to cover those current expenses and then have those expenses adjusted for inflation. Otherwise, when you are retired, you're going to see that your dollar will not go as far every year.

With life expectancy getting longer, some people could be retired for more years than they actually worked.

Memory Lane

	1980	1990	2000	2015
Postage Stamp	$0.15	$0.25	$0.33	$0.49
Annual College Tuition	$3,101	$6,562	$10,820	$20,403
Movie Ticket	$2.69	$4.23	$5.39	$8.12

SOURCES: www.johnstonsarchive.net/other/postage.html; hwww.statisticbrain.com/average-cost-of-college-tuition/; www.boxofficemojo.com/yearly/

Do you remember what the cost of a movie ticket was when you were a kid? Look how little a postage stamp cost back in 1980 and what it is today. It is worth repeating: Inflation is real, prices will increase, and this is a compelling reason to begin investing early so that compounding interest can work for us. The goal is to create enough net worth so that inflation doesn't negatively affect us in retirement.

What's Ahead?

Next we will focus on the execution of your plan, using knowledge of today's investment world to grow, build, protect, and transfer your wealth.

KEY INSIGHTS FROM THIS CHAPTER

- Compound interest is often called the eighth wonder of the world because it has powerful qualities.
- Time can work for you with disciplined savings, proper asset allocation, and a long-term plan.
- There's never a "perfect" time to invest and the cost of procrastination can be significant.
- Start saving and investing early in your life, making it a high priority.
- With life expectancies getting longer, some people could be retired for more years than they actually work.
- In planning for retirement, be sure to adjust expenses for inflation—otherwise you may run out of money.

Note

1. Source: Daniel A. Yergin and Joseph Stanislaw, *The Commanding Heights: The Battle for the World Economy*, (New York: Touchstone, 2002).

Chapter 6

Building Your Wealth

I n order to give you perspective, I want to show you how stocks, bonds, and cash have performed historically. I also want to point out how crucial it is to have the proper asset allocation for your investment portfolio. In this chapter, I will explain all about asset allocation and asset classes including equity, fixed income securities and cash equivalents, the volatility of them all, and how to determine your overall risk tolerance.

Before I begin, let me highlight an interesting study by Joseph Davis, PhD, and Daniel Piquet of Vanguard, an investment company with more than $3 trillion in global assets under management. In 2011, Davis and Piquet wrote a white paper titled "Recessions and Balanced Portfolio Returns." According to their study, since 1926, a diversified investor's overall return didn't dramatically change whether the economic environment was expanding or contracting. As long as the investor had a mix of 50 percent bonds and 50 percent stock, they averaged a return of around 5 percent per year, on a net return basis of factoring in inflation. Of course, past returns are no guarantees for future performance, but it does give an investor a sense of what is potentially reasonable to assume as a rate of return if they are equally diversified in equities and bonds. While past performance is not a guarantee of future results, smart investors in today's modern world might take Mark Twain's well known quote to heart: "History doesn't repeat itself but it often rhymes."

The Financial Engine of Your Wealth Creation

Let's discuss some basics about stocks and bonds because equities (a.k.a. stocks) and fixed income (a.k.a. bonds) should make up the core of your investment portfolio. They are what drive the "financial engine" of your wealth creation automobile and help you achieve your financial goals.

Stocks

By purchasing shares of stock you have the opportunity to own a piece of that company. You share in its profits and its losses. You need to understand that you're not just investing in something to make money immediately—there is a company behind what you're investing in, and you've got to understand what makes it run and how it plans to grow, who is its competition, and what the risks are in making the investment. The biggest risk is that you can lose all of *your* money when investing in a company's stock.

The important thing to know about buying stocks is that you should be investing in them for the long-term, because the potential for growth occurs over years, not days or months. It is not feasible to accurately predict what direction the stock market will go in the short term: Some inexperienced investors pay more attention to what the media is saying about the markets on a particular day than to what is appropriate for them long term. This gets back to what we discussed earlier, if you stick to your plan, you can shut out the noise. You should have a strategy in place, and not one that is driven by what the market did in the past three hours, or what the pundits say will happen tomorrow. It is true that with the world's interconnectedness, bad news travels quickly and the fear from the bad news creates violent negative short-term momentum. For this reason, the portion of your portfolio that is allocated in stocks should be of high quality companies in different sectors and asset classes that have growth and dividend potential. Warren Buffett once said, "If you aren't willing to own a stock for 10 years, don't even think about owning it for 10 minutes. Put together a portfolio of companies whose aggregate earnings march upward over the years, and so also will the portfolio's market value."

Bonds

A bond is basically a loan where you are the lender. The organization that sells a bond is known as the issuer, which can be a company or government. You can think of a bond as an IOU given by a borrower (the issuer) to a lender (you, the investor). Bonds are fixed income instruments. They're supposed to be conservative and are the part of your portfolio intended to be stable although, of course, there will be times when that is not the case. When interest rates go up, the value of bonds will go down. When interest rates go down, the value of bonds will go up. A bond's "duration," measured in years, will help provide a general idea of how the bond will perform based on a changing interest rate environment. It is not exact, but for every percentage point that interest rates rise (or fall), the bond's value will decline (or increase) by its duration. The shorter the duration, the less sensitive that bond is to changing interest rates. Here is an example of how duration works: If rates fall by one percentage point, the Vanguard Total Bond Market index, which currently has a duration of 5.7 percent, would rise by 5.7 percent. Since the fund also pays investors bond interest of 2.1 percent per year, it would post a total return of 7.8 percent. (2.1 percent + 5.7 percent = 7.8 percent). Conversely, if rates were to rise by one percentage point, the fund would lose 3.6 percent (2.1 percent − 5.7 percent = −3.6 percent).

Cash Equivalents

Cash equivalents are assets that can be converted to cash quickly and easily. These securities have a low-risk, low-return profile. They are short-term instruments, have high credit quality (which means there is little risk of default), and are highly liquid. Cash equivalents include U.S. Government Treasury Bills, short-term government bonds, bank certificates of deposit, bank savings accounts, and other money market instruments. Remember, don't expect much return from these types of investments, you are paying for security and liquidity.

Alternative Assets

Recently, there has been a growing interest in alternative assets. Most alternative assets include commodities and other hedging strategies such as options (puts and calls on stocks). A good way to understand hedging is to think of it as insurance. When people decide to hedge, they are insuring themselves against a possible negative event.

When used appropriately, investments in alternative assets can help to minimize risk in an investment portfolio. Unfortunately, due to liquidity issues, when used inappropriately, they could be seen as financial weapons of mass destruction. We will not discuss alternative strategies at great length in this book since my focus is on imparting a sound long-term strategy to help you build the appropriate *money mindset*. However, if you want to learn more about "alts," there are many books on the subject that can offer some appropriate ways of utilizing such instruments.

Asset Allocation

Now that you have a bit more knowledge about stocks (equities), bonds (fixed income), and cash equivalents, it is time to think about allocating the assets in your portfolio. But, you're probably wondering, what exactly is asset allocation? And just what is the appropriate allocation for you? How do you determine it? How much equity and bonds should you own? How much cash or cash equivalents should you hold?

First, asset allocation involves dividing your investment portfolio among your stocks, bonds, cash, and perhaps alternative assets. The asset allocation that works best for you at any given point in your life will depend largely on your time horizon and your ability to tolerate risk.

By including asset categories with investment returns that move up and down under different market conditions within a portfolio, you have the potential to protect against significant losses. The correct asset allocation is the one that helps you to meet your financial goals. This is because you're able to maintain it during most all market conditions and you understand and take into consideration your time horizon. If you are three to five years from retirement with a moderate tolerance for risk, you might split your money evenly between stocks and bonds. But if you are a more conservative investor, you might put only 30 percent in stocks. If you are younger and have a longer time horizon, you might consider anywhere from 60 to 80 percent in stocks for your asset allocation.

Historically, the returns of the four major asset categories have not moved up and down at the same time. Market conditions that cause one asset category to do well often cause another asset category to have average or poor returns. By investing in more than one asset category, you'll reduce the risk that you'll lose money and your portfolio's overall investment returns will have a smoother ride. If one asset category's investment return falls, you'll be in a position to counteract your losses in that asset category with better investment returns in another asset category.[1]

Importance of Asset Allocation

In 1986, Gary P. Brinson, Randolph Hood, and Gilbert L. Bee-bower wrote the paper "Determinants of Portfolio Performance" for *Financial Analyst Journal*. The authors asserted that the asset allocation of a portfolio is the primary determinant of the portfolio's return, with security selection and market timing playing only minor roles in total performance. Their study examined the quarterly returns of 91 large U.S. pension funds from 1974 to 1983. Their conclusion was that 93.6 percent of the variation of return was a result of the portfolio's asset allocation.

Overall, your asset allocation is determined by the amount of risk you can tolerate. Completing a risk tolerance question-naire will help you in your determination.

Here are some sample questions that you might see in a risk tolerance questionnaire. . . .

If your portfolio valued at $50,000 declined in value to $39,000 within one year, what would you likely do?
  A. Sell all the positions and move the money to safer investments.
  B. Sell only the losing investments.
  C. Sell nothing.
  D. Buy more as the losing investment may represent opportunity

If the above portfolio declined by an additional 10 percent to $35,100 the following year, what would you most likely do?
  A. Sell all the positions and avoid investments that fluctuate greatly.
  B. Sell only the losing positions and move the money to safer investments.

C. Keep the same positions.

D. Purchase additional positions as the investments that declined may represent an opportunity.

There are a number of risk tolerance questionnaires available online for free.

Vanguard has a one that you might find helpful, at www.vanguard.com/assetmix.

If you really take the time to understand your risk tolerance and you allocate your portfolio holdings based on how you answer the questions, then you really don't have to be so emotionally susceptible to the gyrations of the markets on a day-to-day basis. You will know that you followed a very methodical process to get to those allocations. The questionnaire helps you think about all of this by using an emotional context. So when you are in an environment where the markets are quite volatile, you can feel confident sticking to your strategy. In a calm environment, you will have already thought about your potential actions and reactions in a potentially emotional situation; basically, the risk tolerance questionnaire helps you determine at what point in a market decline your portfolio becomes too volatile for your own personal risk tolerance, risk capacity, and risk perception.

Once you have gone through the risk assessment process, you can rest assured you're allocated appropriately. I suggest that you revisit the risk tolerance questionnaire regularly to update and keep yourself focused. If your new answers lead you to feel that you need to be a bit more conservative with your investments, then you can adjust your investments with confidence. Remember, the key is to look at the end game and recognize there is almost always going to be volatility in the short term.

The odds of benefiting long term from the capital markets are best when you understand the logic of asset allocation, complete a risk tolerance questionnaire, and then diversify accordingly.

If you follow this process, then during emotional moments you won't fall prey to a knee-jerk reaction. It is in those moments of great emotion when you can become your own worst enemy. Sometimes, you might need an advisor to hold your hand and help you through those times, and/or you can go back to your plan and make sure that you're still on target.

What Does Salsa Have to Do with Asset Allocation?

Let me tell you a story about why asset allocation is like making salsa.

I heard Craig Israelsen, PhD, a Personal Finance Professor at Brigham Young University, speak about his approach to asset allocation. His explanation is unforgettable. He said that asset allocation is a lot like making salsa. So, for the ingredients you're going to have tomatoes, onions, cilantro, lime, spices, and some jalapeno peppers. Each ingredient is unique and different. Yet, when you have the right proportions and you blend them together as a group, it takes on a wonderful new flavor. If you taste the salsa, it's difficult to discern the tomato, the lime, or the jalapeno pepper. When mixing the ingredients, they become entirely new. The jalapeno pepper could be the equivalent of alternative assets in your portfolio. You don't want too much jalapeno pepper because you won't be able to taste the other flavors and it could set your mouth on fire. That's the beauty of a good salsa. It's simple, yet distinguishable and flavorful. But, with too much of any one ingredient, it really can take away from the balance of the perfect salsa that it could be. If it's too hot, you're not going to want to taste it again. Investors want to not have too much jalapeno pepper in their portfolio and have a nice mix of tomatoes, onions, and other ingredients.

Okay, enough about salsa. Let's go back to the basics of financial success: You must have a strong offensive strategy that will make you money for the long term. You can use your more defensive strategies where you're trying very hard to preserve your gains. A strong offense wins games, but a strong defense wins championships.

What it comes down to is that the right asset allocation will help your plan be successful. If the plan is too aggressive, all it takes is one major market correction and you will probably no longer buy into the concept of investing in equities (stocks). If you are not aggressive enough, your portfolio won't benefit from compound interest as it normally would, and the portfolio is just not going to grow as it needs to grow in order to help you reach your goals.

It is really important to have balance in the portfolio. With bonds, you have those built-in shock absorbers that help your defensive strategy and give you a much smoother ride. Even though we all know that there are going to be potholes in the road, by having a good mix of stocks and bonds in your overall portfolio mix, the ride will still be tolerable.

Rebalancing Your Portfolio

Rebalancing is really a forced way to incorporate the "buy low, sell high" mantra. For example, if you had $100,000 and 70 percent of that money was allocated to stocks, 20 percent in bonds; and 10 percent in cash, it might be that the next year that $100,000 grows to $150,000 but the growth was from the bonds. Since the bonds appreciated in value, that takes the asset allocation that you had determined based on the risk tolerance questionnaire, and throws the balance of investments out of whack (the problem would be that now your asset allocation is out of balance). Being out of balance could mean that if the markets are going up, you could miss out on the upside; if the markets are down, you may lose more than you thought you could. So it is important to always make sure that you're rebalancing back to your risk level.

In the previous example, rebalancing forces you to sell those bonds at a profit, and then take the profits and reinvest them back into the asset class that underperformed. So, in essence, you're forcing yourself to buy low.

Investors should consider rebalancing annually regardless of what happens in their lives. If you have a life-altering event such as a death, a promotion, or job loss, you would be wise to complete a new risk tolerance questionnaire. If your life has shifted and your situation is much different than it was before, it might mean you are in a position to take on more risk (or less). For example, if you are retiring, you may need to take on less risk. So, by redoing the risk tolerance questionnaire, you essentially reassess the appropriate allocation based on your life after that major event.

It's actually quite simple to rebalance. Many times, 401(k)s allow you to rebalance your portfolio quarterly or annually. If you work with a financial advisor, he or she may already be rebalancing for you. So, it can be as easy as checking a box and saying, "Okay, rebalance my portfolio annually or quarterly." That way it's automated and you know that your portfolio will never deviate too much from where it needs to align with your long-term goals.

Measuring Volatility

But let's not forget about volatility and how it can be measured. Of course, the higher the volatility, the riskier the investment. Beta is one of many measurement tools that helps evaluate past volatility or the systematic risk of an investment. It does this by measuring the volatility of a portfolio relative to the S&P 500, which is one of the most commonly followed equity indices (many consider it one of the best representations of the U.S. stock market and a bellwether for the U.S. economy). So, for measuring beta, or volatility, the S&P 500 in this case is the benchmark, which always carries a beta of 1. Most financial professionals consider the S&P 500 to be an aggressive investment. For example, in 2008 (which was during the great banking and mortgage crisis) the S&P 500 lost approximately 37 percent of its value in just one calendar year. If investors decide that they do not want to potentially lose that much of their value in one calendar year, I might suggest then that the beta of their portfolio should be less than 1. If someone had a beta of .8, it would mean that they carried 80 percent of the risk of the S&P 500. Another way of saying this is that an investor who carried a beta of .8 had 20 percent less risk than the S&P 500. Whereas, if someone has a beta of 1.2, it means that they have 20 percent more volatility, which means they will go up 20 percent more, but they'll go down 20 percent more than the stock market as measured by the S&P 500 index.

More times than I can count, investors have told me that they consider themselves to be conservative investors. With a response like that, I immediately think of a beta that's less than 1, but sometimes as I'm calculating an investor's beta, it turns out that their beta is greater than 1. Unfortunately, there's a disconnect between what they're telling me (conservative investor) and how their investments are allocated (aggressive investor). Make sure that, if you are conservative, your investments are allocated accordingly. This is one of the many reasons to use a risk-tolerance questionnaire as a self-assessment and clarity tool.

How do you reduce market risk in your portfolio? One of the best ways to lower the beta of a portfolio is by adding cash and bonds.

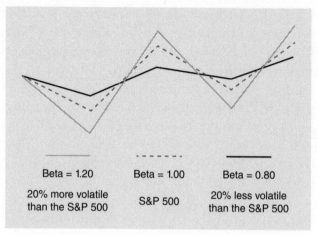

Beta Chart

My father taught me that we diversify not to make more, but to protect what we have already made.

Sometimes a client might say to me, "I know someone whose investment portfolio earned 30 percent last year. Why am I not getting that kind of return?" My respectful response is usually, "Well, we don't know how they are investing, nor do we know how much risk they are exposed to in order to capture that type of return. We know that you're investing based on your overall plan, which we have calculated and have, in essence, solved for how much you need to be contributing and at what type of return you should be earning with the lowest amount of risk possible." The goal is to maximize your risk-adjusted return. At this point, you might be thinking: "That beta thing makes sense; I should know how much risk I am currently exposed to." Great news: You can go to www.morningstar.com and type in the ticker symbol of almost all publicly traded securities. Morningstar has already done the calculation for you and will tell you what the beta is for that specific investment. This helps you with each individual investment in your portfolio, but won't give you your *overall* beta level, which is where a financial planner often comes into play.

Warren Buffett, one of the most respected and publicly known investors, wisely said, "Never test the depth of the river with both feet." Apply this metaphor to the way you think about your investments and how you build your portfolio. It is just too risky to test the level of risk in your portfolio by trial and error.

Be Smart about Recovery Times

I often tell my clients that it is easy to make money during a bull market—a rising tide lifts all boats. The art of wealth management is attempting to minimize losses in the down years. The deeper the hole, the more it will take to recover. This is one reason to consider the benefits of constructing a low volatility portfolio. Instead of embracing investments that are prone to large swings up and down due to various economic and market factors, it might be better to embrace investments that are less prone to wild up and down swings. The goal here would be to create steady growth via market gains and the magic of compounding interest.

Many people may do the mental math that if their investment declines 50 percent, they need only to make 50 percent to get back to even. Unfortunately, that is not how compound interest works. In reality, the investor would have to see a 100 percent gain to fully recover from his or her loss. Here's an example: Imagine you invested $100,000, then subsequently that $100,000 declined by 50 percent and was then valued at only $50,000. In order to recover the original investment, the investment will now need to appreciate 100 percent to get back to $100,000. For this reason, there needs to be great mindfulness of how quickly things can decline in the current environment.

Gain Required to Break Even

If You Lose	Gain Required to Break Even
10%	11%
20%	25%
30%	43%
40%	67%
50%	100%
75%	300%
90%	900%

Dollar Cost Averaging

Now that you have determined your asset allocation, how those various securities or asset classes have performed historically, and how much you should be putting away on a monthly basis, then you should consider dollar cost averaging every month. Dollar cost averaging is a strategy for buying a fixed dollar amount of a particular investment on a regular schedule, regardless of the share price. As a result, more shares are purchased when prices are low, and fewer shares are bought when prices are high. So, *dollar cost averaging allows you to minimize the effect of timing the market (trying to time the market is something I typically advise against).* When the markets are down and you're buying, you're accumulating more shares. You get a better average share cost when buying at the highs, and you acquire more shares when buying at the lows. If a client says, "I've got $2 million; I want you to manage it. It is, right now, all in cash." I might respond, "Well let's put this $2 million to work in a diversified investment portfolio, but let's stream in the cash over six months, not all at once." The first month we put one-sixth of the money to work in this allocation, the second month we put the second tranche of the sixth in that same allocation. Then we put the dollars to work over six months, so we're dollar cost averaging in; we're getting the advantages of both the highs and the lows and we are thus more safely entering into the market.

Systematic Withdrawals

Let's assume that you followed your plan, contributed what was needed over many years, earned the appropriate return, plus allowed the plan time to grow to a point where you are able to retire. Congratulations, you now have enough money working for you that you can downshift into retirement. Now what? What is the best way to transition from a saver to spender? How do you begin to live off your investments?

One solid source of retirement income for many individuals is a systematic withdrawal program from an investment portfolio. A systematic withdrawal program allows you to receive a specified amount of money each month. These programs also allow you to continue participating in the potential rewards of your investments while receiving monthly income.

People understand that they need to take income from their investments. Sometimes they may think they only want to take out interest. In an ideal world that would be just fine, but every month the value of their net worth is going to be changing. If you're investing in equities that are not dividend producing, the upside potential is growth. It's a good idea to determine a percentage that is realistic to withdraw and then systematically take out the money on which you need to live. Some years, you might be building a surplus, and some years you might be creating a deficit, but on average you would just be taking out enough to comfortably live. The goal is to keep your principle capital at work. In times of difficulty, you may decide to temporarily spend less. As Ben Franklin often said: "A penny saved is a penny earned."

Where Does Real Estate Fit In?

It is true that an important, and, at times, the largest component of your net worth could be held in real estate. For most people, however, their real estate investments will be limited to their primary residence. *Money Mindset* is about ways to create wealth that can translate into income upon retirement.

In a way, I look at the equity in your home as sacred money. We do not want to factor and calculate those dollars for retirement income purposes. It is true that at some point you might downsize your home and use the excess dollars after a transaction like that. At that point, you can factor those dollars into your equation, but until then, look at your home as a sanctuary from the world, not as a short-term investment.

With that being said, when it comes to mortgages, I usually recommend going with a 15- or 30-year fixed mortgage. It may be higher than an adjustable rate mortgage but at least you do not have to worry about the payment potentially going up in the future. Being able to budget around a fixed housing cost is very beneficial.

Of course there are other ways investors can invest in real estate; including buying real estate and then renting it out for income, as well as investing in REITs (real estate investment trusts). These strategies can be lucrative, given certain economic environments if executed appropriately. If executed inappropriately, especially in the area of excess leverage, the investment can have damaging ramifications to your financial situation.

What's Ahead?

In the next chapter, we'll discuss taxes and insurance. It's important for each of us to know the tax system, how we are each affected, and what we are obligated to pay. Insurance protects a person or entity from extreme financial loss or responsibility due to an unfortunate emergency, accident, or negative unforeseen event.

KEY INSIGHTS FROM THIS CHAPTER

- It is crucial to have the proper asset allocation for your investment portfolio. Stocks and bonds should be the core of your investment portfolio.
- Asset allocation of a portfolio is the primary determinant of the portfolio's return. Security selection and market timing play only minor roles in total performance.
- If you really take the time to understand the risk tolerance questionnaire and you appropriately allocate your portfolio holdings based on how you answer the questions, then you are not emotionally susceptible to the gyrations of the markets on a day-to-day basis.
- Rebalancing is really a forced way to incorporate the "buy low, sell high" mantra.
- The higher the volatility, the riskier the investment.
- It is easy to make money during a bull market—a rising tide lifts all boats. The art of wealth management is attempting to minimize losses in the down years.
- Dollar cost averaging and systematic withdrawal programs are good strategies.

Note

1. "Beginner's Guide to Asset Allocation, Diversification, and Rebalancing," U.S. Securities and Exchange Commission, www.sec.gov/investor/pubs/assetallocation.htm.

Chapter 7

Taxes and Insurance

Taxes

Understanding how taxes have been used to support civilizations over the course of modern history can help you realize how important they are to us today as U.S. citizens. While some people may take the viewpoint that fewer taxes or more taxes is better, the following summary will help you as you sift through your own opinions about taxes and the benefits to our society.

Did you know that the earliest income tax was implemented in Mesopotamia over 4,500 years ago, where people paid taxes throughout the year in the form of livestock? The ancient world also had estate taxes, or "death taxes." The earliest recorded evidence of a death tax comes from ancient Egypt, where they charged a 10 percent tax on property transferred at the time of death in 700 B.C.[1]

Since then, the way we pay taxes has changed significantly. However, some ancient taxes still persist in the modern world.

In 2006, China eliminated what was the oldest still-existing tax in history. An agricultural tax was created 2,600 years ago and was eliminated in order to help improve the well-being of rural farmers in China. In the United States, the tax system evolved dramatically during the nation's history. The federal government first imposed income taxes in 1861 to help pay for the Civil War.

Before the 1860s, the government got by on taxing imports and exports. But with the significant cost of the Civil War burdening the treasury, the government enacted a tax rate of 3 percent on incomes above $800, and 5 percent for incomes above $10,000. These measures were short-lived, and the laws were repealed in 1872. American citizens didn't pay income taxes for the next 20 years.

With the onset of World War I, the federal government again needed to raise revenue quickly, and in 1918, legislators raised the rates sharply, particularly on high-income citizens: 77 percent on incomes over $1 million. The marginal tax rate went down slowly over the following 20 years, but it went back up during the Great Depression, since fewer people had any taxable income.

As the nation emerged from the Depression, the New Deal brought new benefits for citizens—and a new type of tax. In 1937, under the Roosevelt administration, Congress ratified the Federal Insurance Contributions Act (FICA), and FICA taxes funded the Social Security Administration. When Medicare passed in 1965 under the Johnson administration, FICA taxes increased to cover program costs. FICA is a flat tax, a standard percentage that everyone pays up to a set maximum. But income taxes are subject to various changes at different income levels. The marginal tax rate stayed high all the way through World War II, when it went as high as 92 percent. (It has continued to go down over the years to a low of 31 percent in 1992, and it now stands at 35 percent.)

During World War II, the new tax policy added a feature that we accept as routine these days: income tax withholding. Before World War II, most people paid their entire tax bill on the tax due date, which put a significant strain on the government's bank account. To end the feast-or-famine effect on the nation's coffers, payroll-withholding laws have evolved and now require citizens to pay at least 90 percent of expected taxes due by the end of the year.[2]

Our taxes pay for education, roads, and national defense, among many other things. As our population has gotten older, more and more of our overall budget funds entitlement programs like Social Security. Those costs are only going to continue to rise, yet we have fewer taxpayers in the system. The reality is that as America's age wave has hit, a higher percentage today is going to the entitlement programs.

Total Federal Spending 2015: $3.84 Trillion

Social Security, unemployment and labor	$1.28 trillion	33%
Medicare and health	$1.05 trillion	27%
Military	$609.3 billion	16%
Interest on debt	$229.2 billion	6%
Veterans benefits	$160.6 billion	4%
Food and agriculture	$135.7 billon	3%
Education	$102.3 billon	3%
Transportation	$85 billion	3%
Housing and community	$65.5 billion	2%
International affairs	$50.2 billion	1%
Energy and environment	$44.8 billion	1%
Science	$29.8 billion	1%

SOURCE: OMB National Priorities Project.

The bottom line is that it is important for each of us to know the tax system, how we are personally affected, and what we are obligated to pay. We don't need to have Uncle Sam as an active participant in our lives; we just need to abide by the current tax system. Too many people try to pay less in taxes and try to figure out all the schemes to game the system. But, seriously, that really shouldn't be the way we look at taxes. Taxes are necessary, plain and simple. Think of it this way: The more you pay, the more fortunate you are overall. Don't spend your time and energy on tax loopholes because they might catch up to you and won't benefit you as you had hoped. Just understand the tax code, or hire a Certified Public Accountant, and pay what is required of you. Pay the piper and move forward with your life.

We all recognize that there is a cost to infrastructure and to the many things that makes a society function well. Ben Franklin said that in this world nothing is certain except death and taxes. That is why you must research your personal situation, and determine what sections of the tax code apply to you, especially when you look at your retirement planning.

Of course, you should not pay more taxes than is really fair or due from you. Arthur Godfrey famously said, "I am proud to pay taxes in the United States. The only thing is, I could be just as proud for half of the money." The point here is to pay your fair share and be proud that you did.

How to Calculate Your Effective Tax Rate

Most people are familiar with the marginal tax rates, the rate at which your income is taxed for each tax bracket in which you qualify. However, more important is your effective tax rate, which is the actual percentage of your income you are actually paying to the IRS.

So, how do you calculate your effective tax rate? The following three steps may help out.

1. Take your total income from all sources, including interest, capital gains, and dividends (Form 1040), and add any other amounts received, but not required, to be reported to the IRS.

2. Now look at the total income taxes paid that year.

3. Divide the taxes paid by total income.

I suggest that you work with a skilled CPA who can look at maximizing your tax deductions and credits, and utilizing the tax code to your benefit while staying within the confines of the law.

Judge Learned Hand, United States District Court for the Southern District of New York and, later, the United States Court of Appeals for the Second Circuit, may have said it best: "Anyone may arrange his affairs so that his taxes shall be as low as possible. He is not bound to choose that pattern which best pays the treasury. There is not even a patriotic duty to increase one's taxes."

Insurance

We all recognize that there is randomness in life. Sometimes bad things happen that we can't foresee. If there is a possible financial loss that could be so astronomical that it could destroy a person's security, then the risk should be transferred to a third party. In those situations, it is important to transfer that risk to another entity, like an insurance company, so they can manage the risk with a larger pool of individuals.

In this section, we'll talk about managing risk. Properly managing the risks in your life will provide a solid foundation for your overall financial plan. Failure to manage risks can jeopardize all other aspects of your finances, including your investments and retirement plans.

The first step in the risk management process is identifying areas in your life that might cause you to experience a financial loss. The second step is determining how to manage those risks.

There are four methods of handling risk:

1. Retain risk: You choose to bear the full financial burden in the event of a loss.
2. Reduce risk: You restrict the conditions that can create a loss.
3. Avoid risk: You decide not to participate in risk-creating activities.
4. Transfer risk: You purchase insurance to help cover a loss

If you can't afford to replace it, if it were to be lost, damaged, or destroyed, then you should explore ways to transfer the risk.

For an example: Let's say that a student works all summer to save up for a laptop for school. Upon buying the laptop, the vender asks if he would like to protect the purchase by insuring it. If the student is in a financial position where they could not afford to replace the laptop if it were to be damaged, he or she may want to consider paying a little extra to buy protection.

If, on the other hand, the laptop were to be damaged and the cost of buying a new laptop would not create financial hardship, then you are better off retaining, reducing, or avoiding certain activities, as opposed to transferring the risk by buying the protection plan.

In this book, I am going to focus on the last risk. While the first three methods are potential options, transferring risk offers a level of protection that the other three just cannot in most cases. Transferring risk means buying insurance: health insurance, life insurance, disability insurance, or auto insurance. On a macro basis, insurance companies manage a pool of risk by collecting premiums and quantifying how many claims they will have to pay out. They run their numbers to determine the premium they need to charge based on the frequency of a loss in order to have enough reserves to pay when that loss takes place while still collecting a premium and profiting.

Let's talk about six kinds of insurance and the ways you can use them as part of building your financial foundation. We will talk about health insurance, long-term care insurance, life insurance, disability insurance, auto insurance, and homeowner's insurance.

Health Insurance

As we all know, health insurance is an important topic and issue today. If an individual doesn't have health insurance and is diagnosed with a terminal illness, they could have millions of dollars set aside, yet their treatment could potentially exhaust their entire savings and investment accounts. So, it's crucial to have enough health insurance to protect against a catastrophic illness.

Many people rely on employer-sponsored health insurance plans, but often you still need to have savings set aside for health expenses with the rise of high-deductible health care plans. These types of plans require greater out-of-pocket payments as employers shift the increasing burden of health costs onto their employees.

No one plans to get sick or hurt, but most people need medical care at some point. Health insurance covers these costs and offers many other important benefits. Now more than ever before people have options for health insurance to protect their finances should medical emergencies or issues arise.

Long-Term Care Insurance

When it comes to long-term care insurance, we recognize that more and more people in their lifetimes will most likely find themselves in an assisted living facility, or in need of a caregiver to help them with their day-to-day activities. That can be a great financial burden to absorb. It may be wise, especially if dementia or Alzheimer's runs in the family, to consider having at least a long-term care policy that can pay a small dollar amount per day for your care.

I tell clients that in retirement, there are three stages: The go-go years, the slow-go years, and the no-go years. During the go-go years, you will be spending your time and energy on everything that you wanted to do in life but did not have the time or money for. These will be your peak spending years in retirement. I often hear from clients that their go-go years are some of the most enjoyable years of their lives. Every day is a Saturday and they can spend every second doing whatever fulfills them as an individual.

Then you may slowly transition into the slow-go years. Still people are active during this time period, it's just they are not moving as fast. It becomes much more about quality of time, rather than quantity.

Last comes the no-go years. It is during this time period that we want to appropriately assess your physical and mental needs and plan for your care. Spending in all areas, except healthcare, slows down dramatically during the no-go years. It is during this time period that having a long-term care policy may make sense. It can help with the costs of your day-to-day care. From bathing to feeding to cleaning to cooking, inside a facility or at home, a long-term care policy can reduce the monthly financial hardship that this stage of your life can present. It is wise to not assume that a long-term care policy will cover all your costs; that is unrealistic. Instead you should look at a long-term care policy to take the edge off the financial burden and keep your finances in the black.

For many people younger than 50, long-term care insurance seems like something to defer to the future. But similar to a term life insurance policy, the earlier you lock in a long-term policy, the less it will cost over the long haul. Another incentive to start young with long-term care is the greater likelihood you'll qualify. The requirements get stricter and the policies get more expensive as you age. The best way to make the decision as to when to buy long-term care insurance is to have an honest dialogue with your financial planner.

In some cases, individuals may have enough in assets to become self-insured. In this scenario, even factoring in the cost of your day-to-day care would be less than the amount of income your assets are producing for you on a regular basis. As I mentioned at the beginning of the chapter, if you can manage and control the costs of this stage of your retirement without needing insurance, then the need to transfer that risk is not present.

Life Insurance

If you are the primary breadwinner and/or have small children at home, your spouse and children could have great financial difficulty if you pass away unexpectedly. To safeguard against this possibility, you need to have insurance coverage substantial enough to cover the mortgage, putting the kids through school, and other expenses to ensure your family can maintain their lifestyle.

Research from Voya Financial's "Voya Retire Ready Index" found that only 18 percent of workers have more than $500,000 in total life insurance coverage. When you think about what it would cost to replace your income and support a family over many years, this generally is not nearly enough to ensure financial security.[3]

Your family will be suffering emotionally and you don't want them to suffer financially at the same time. You pay the premium for life insurance and have the reassurance that if something happens to you, there would be enough money coming into the household federal- and state-tax-free to help your family continue moving forward financially.

As your need to cover expenses goes down, the need for life insurance may also go down. Conversely, if your expenses go up, your life insurance needs will increase as well. That's really the essence of it. You may need life insurance while the children are young, but the need may decrease as your children age and you have more savings and fewer expenses to cover. Simply, you buy insurance when you can't afford to replace that which might be irreplaceable.

Types of Life Insurance

There are two types of life insurance: cash value policies and term insurance. The trick is to decide which type is best for you.

Term life insurance has no cash value. Your premium payments pay for the cost of the insurance, and your beneficiaries will receive a lump sum payment (called a death benefit) only if you die. You pay the premiums for a period of time and are covered during that term (thus the word "term" life insurance). As retirement approaches, your need for life insurance is likely to decline, as children become able to support themselves and retirement savings come into play. At a certain point, you can drop your term insurance without penalty. Because there is no cash value component, term life insurance premiums are typically lower than cash value premiums.

On the other hand, cash value policies fall into a different camp than term life insurance and serve an additional and valuable purpose. These policies are permanent in nature and the cost of insurance is based on your entire life expectancy. Here is how it works: You make a payment every month for the cost of the insurance, and there is an extra amount going into a separate account that creates cash value for you. The cash value portion of the policy can become a valuable and flexible financial tool for you after it accumulates. In many cases, the cash value can be borrowed against and paid off eventually at your death, when the life insurance death benefit is paid out. The borrowed money is subtracted from the death benefit, creating a nontaxable exchange.

Remember that cash value policies are typically more expensive than term insurance. When you buy term insurance, you're covering your liability for a specific number of years. After those years have been completed, the term insurance expires and then you either go without insurance or have to buy a new insurance policy.

Some individuals look at life insurance begrudgingly, and don't want to consider it an investment. They want to pay the least amount for coverage. They know they'll need that coverage for the next 15 or 20 years as their kids are getting older, or until they determine they have enough money to be financially independent. If this sounds like you, you may lean toward buying term life insurance. As one's net worth increases and expenses decrease, the need for life insurance *may* decrease as well.

Disability Insurance

What would you do if you were not able to work for three months? Six months? A year? Longer? This is a scary prospect for any professional. Disability insurance helps protect against financial loss due to an inability to work, offering income protection against injury, illness, or any condition that might cause physical impairment or incapacity to work.

If an individual owns his or her own business and is worried about the possibility of becoming disabled, there is an option of buying a disability policy that will pay while the business owner is not able to work. I work with a client who is a successful doctor who runs his own family practice. His staff, family, and patients depend on him to be healthy and to be able to work.

In his case, he purchased a disability policy that can keep his business operating if he were to become disabled. It would also pay him a specific dollar amount per month until he reaches full retirement age.

Americans use insurance to protect a host of assets, from cars to homes to jewelry. But many people forget to insure their most important asset—the ability to work and earn a living. Social Security states that, "Just over one in four of today's 20-year-olds will become disabled before reaching age 67." And if disease or injury renders you disabled early in your working life, the lost wages can be worth much more than a house or a sedan.

While the Social Security Administration does provide a small amount of disability benefits as a safety net, it is a small amount of help and will likely not be enough to cover your shortfall needs. In addition, there is a complex eligibility process, and benefits apply to Americans with a medical condition that prevents them from working for at least 12 months. If the prospect of losing just a few months' income or living on a fraction of your paycheck just isn't an option, you will want to seek out some form of disability insurance to protect yourself. Your employer (or your spouse's employer) may offer a group disability insurance plan or you could research and secure an individual disability plan. Start by speaking with your human resources department or benefits coordinator at work. If you are self-employed, then go online and research individual policy options or speak with your financial planner.

Automobile Insurance

The law now requires that every car has its own insurance policy, if for no other reason than to protect other people from your mistakes. Of course, you can get more comprehensive coverage that protects you from other people's mistakes. In other words, this means protection against the underinsured and the noninsured, which is crucial. Of course, within the auto policy, the coverage helps with the repairs of the car after the deductible is satisfied.

Automobile insurance companies will be aggressive in competing for your business, and while the process of comparing cost and benefits might feel overwhelming at times, it is important to sift through your options and decide if the lowest cost provider is the best way to go. There is no one right solution and no single best insurance provider. Your driving record, age, gender, where you live, what kind of car you drive, and many other factors affect your premium. As a starting point, do your research online and ask each insurance carrier what kind of discounts they will give you based on the factors noted above. Also consider the carrier's payment record (some are known to throw up road blocks and deny or draw out the claims process). Others have a history of raising a driver's premiums after just one claim. Use online forums such as Yelp or Angie's List to learn from other people's experiences.

Renters or Homeowner's Insurance

Renters or homeowner's insurance is also called hazard insurance. This is a type of property insurance that covers a private residence. It is an insurance policy that combines various personal insurance protections, which can include losses occurring to one's home, its contents, loss of use (additional living expenses), or loss of other personal possessions of the renter/homeowner, as well as liability insurance for accidents that may happen at the home or at the hands of the homeowner within the policy territory.[4]

Usually within the homeowner's insurance there is a limited liability umbrella policy. You could buy a million-dollar umbrella policy that would cover most types of liability. If a friend or neighbor jumped on your trampoline, fell, and broke their arm, or slipped and fell on your icy steps, your policy would help cover any costs associated with those accidents. An umbrella policy is quite cost-effective. The insurance carrier wants to make sure that you are not at fault if you get sued. If you are at fault, then the insurance carrier must pay that claim. What's interesting is when someone has an umbrella policy and there is some type of suit filed against them (i.e., auto accident) and the insurance is maxed out from the auto insurance, the excess may flow into the umbrella policy.

In case of a claim, insurance carriers will have their own attorneys investigate the case with the hope that they don't have to pay more than necessary. Many times, when people have an umbrella policy, they also receive the legal support from the insurance carrier providing that insurance. That's really quite important. Unfortunately, we live in an environment where some people just want to take from what others have built. And, in a litigious society, some are "sue happy." You really must have an adequate amount of insurance to protect yourself against the world.

Deductibles

Deductibles, in essence, lower the cost of the insurance itself. The higher your deductible, the lower your premiums will be. Using the example of an automobile insurance policy, let's say you have a deductible of $500 on all of your vehicles. You pay the heavy premium to have that low deductible. So, the first $500 is out of your pocket and then everything above that the insurance carrier will pick up. Using this theoretical scenario, think about this: If you were to get into a little fender bender and you backed up into someone, you would be liable for it. You have a deductible of $500, but the damage was $750. Would you submit that claim?" You might think to yourself, "Well, if I submit that claim, the first $500 comes out of my pocket, so then the insurance company will pay $250."

Usually there is a very real possibility that your premium may increase because of the accident. Insurance carriers figure that if you're in one accident, the probability of you being in another accident is now higher. So, then you may think, "Well, I don't want to pay a higher premium just because they're helping me with $250." So, you may need to consider at what point you need to transfer the risk to the insurance company, then raise your deductible to that point. Think of it this way: with a deductible of $500, you may be paying for insurance that you will never use.

Overinsured or Underinsured?

Some people are overinsured and have far too much insurance based on their needs and liabilities, although this is not the common situation. Other times, and more often, people can be completely underinsured. In order to determine how much coverage you need, you should quantify your expenses. If you are insured appropriately, you don't have to be afraid of your own shadow. You can go out and live your life. If you do suffer a catastrophic event, you can be assured, at least financially, that you won't be alone and you will have the support you need in a difficult time.

You can look at insurance policies as being like the side rails on a bridge. If there were no side rails on a bridge, we all probably would be driving across the bridge at one or two miles an hour. If there are side rails on the bridge, then we know that we would have to hit that side rail pretty hard for us to go off the bridge and hurt ourselves. It just gives us enough support and enough structure so we don't focus on the dangers of driving on the bridge, but rather on getting to the other side.

A Defensive Strategy

In Chapter 6, we talked about asset allocation and how bonds can be a defensive strategy when included as a part of an investment portfolio. One could look at insurance as part of a defensive strategy for the rest of your life. You have insurance coverage in place to help your financial situation in those unfortunate situations where you are exposed or liable. By having adequate insurance you are, in essence, protecting your net worth and your family in case you are exposed to the unfavorable randomness of life.

What's Ahead?

In the next chapter, we'll talk about transferring the assets we don't use during our lifetimes to loved ones and/or other beneficiaries.

KEY INSIGHTS FROM THIS CHAPTER

- Transferring risk means buying insurance: health insurance, life insurance, disability insurance, or auto insurance.
- Think of your insurance policies as the side rails on a bridge. If there were no side rails on a bridge, we all probably would be driving across the bridge at one or two miles an hour.
- The first step in the risk management process is identifying areas in your life that might cause you to experience a financial loss.

Notes

1. "Tax History, the Definition of Income Taxes, a Taxucation," Efile, www.efile.com/tax-history-and-the-tax-code/.
2. "United States Tax History: Federal Income Tax History in United States," Money Crashers, www.moneycrashers.com/US-tax-history-federal-income-tax-america/.
3. "Voya Retire Ready Index™," Voya Financial, http://corporate.voya.com/newsroom/media-kits/voya-retire-ready-index.
4. *A Consumer's Guide to Home Insurance,* www.insurance.insureuonline.org/consumer_guide_home.pdf.

Chapter 8

Estate Planning

In this chapter, we'll talk about transferring the assets we don't use during our lifetimes to loved ones and/or other beneficiaries.

Estate planning, in its simplest form, could be defined as how you want to transfer your "stuff" after you've passed away. Leaving a legacy and giving heirs the best platform to succeed in their lives is a meaningful estate planning goal. But, remember what Warren Buffett, one of the world's richest men, said when he was quoted in *Fortune* magazine in 1986: "One should leave enough money to your kids so they can do anything, but not enough so they can do nothing."

Assets pass at death by contract (e.g., beneficiary and transfer on death designations), by law (e.g., beneficiary deed, joint accounts, trusts), and through probate (e.g., testate, or "by will," or intestate, or "no will"). Every adult, whether they have a high net worth or a balance sheet that is negative, has something they want to pass down after death (sometimes it is only their values, not their valuables; sometimes it is both their values and their valuables).

ᴐle Estate Planning Documents

 ıal, regardless of net worth, should consider having these four documents:

1. Last will and testament
2. Durable power of attorney
3. Living will (a.k.a. health care proxy, advanced directive, medical power of attorney)
4. Ethical will

Last Will and Testament

A last will and testament states an individual's wishes. Everyone should have one of these. A last will and testament is used to distribute property to beneficiaries, specify last wishes, and name guardians for minor children. It is an important part of any estate plan. Without one, the courts will make these critical decisions for you. One function of a probate court is proving whether a will exists and helping to settle an estate, especially if there is a third-party interest involved with the estate. I believe everyone needs to have a last will and testament.

If your financial situation is not complex, there are many different avenues you can explore to create an estate planning document. Some individuals, through their employer, might have access to prepaid legal aid and, for a small fee, they could have access to a team of attorneys that would do their estate planning documents at no cost with membership in this prepaid legal. This is a very cost-effective way of getting estate planning documents, as long as one doesn't need a lot of customization. There are also online services like LegalZoom.com and RocketLawyer.com that offer various templates.

Here in Arizona, where I live, the state accepts holographic wills, which means they are handwritten and, with the original signature of the individual, this document will be recognized in the probate court. To find out if your state allows handwritten wills, just do a quick search online.

Durable Power of Attorney

Durable Power of Attorney documents are also important. I also suggest that everyone should have one of these.

Having a durable power of attorney means you're authorizing someone to act on your behalf until the day you pass away.

I currently have a female client who, prior to our professional relationship, was unaware of the importance of having estate planning documents. Unfortunately, her husband began exhibiting signs of dementia and it progressed fairly quickly. Consequently, she was powerless because everything was in his name. She had to go through the process of getting a court order. Not only did it take almost a year to obtain it, it cost her more than five figures in attorney's fees, courts fees, and so on. Most of the costs and the time and energy spent could have been avoided if the couple had consulted an estate planning attorney early on about these important issues.

The Living Will

The other thing everyone needs is a living will. A living will states whether you wish to be resuscitated or if you are want to be kept alive, even in a vegetative state. This document is essential so that your preferences are followed when you cannot speak for yourself.

The Ethical Will

You may also consider creating an ethical will. You might want to write a "love letter" to your kin and other special people in your life. This is sometimes called an "ethical will." While it is not a legal document, it can be a powerful way to express your sentiments and wishes for those you leave behind. Just do an online search for "ethical wills" and you will find many resources.

Beyond the Basics: A Living Trust

The more someone has to give away after their passing, especially if there are businesses involved or minor children, the more they may need a living trust. The reason is that if you only have a last will and testament and you have minor children, there could be a scenario in which anytime your children need to gain access to the estate, and they're under age 18, they may have to go through the court system to get approval. Not only can that be a bottleneck, but it can be time-consuming and costly when you're factoring in attorney's fees.

If you have a living trust in place, that living trust can be the owner of most all your assets. But it cannot own your IRA or your 401(k). An IRA has to be owned by an individual because it is an *Individual* Retirement Account, of course (similarly, the 401(k) is an individual retirement account held within an employer plan, so it cannot be held within a living trust). But any type of property, after-tax accounts, or bank accounts can be titled in the name of the trust. And what's nice about that is, when appropriately titled in the name of the trust, those assets in the trust do not have to go through the probate system.

The probate system is actually a public record, so if there were some business relationships that went sour or if there are family challenges with divorces, remarriages, stepchildren, and so on, there is a record of the individual's intention. The probate system is such that there is also a time period for people to go forward in front of the courts and stake a claim on a person's estate if they feel that it is appropriate to do so.

Conversely, a living trust is *not* a public record, so you would be able to bypass the public record aspect and keep it all in-house within the trustees of the living trust. This can provide a nice level of privacy for the family as well. My wife and I are cotrustees of our living trust and if something were to happen to me as a trustee, she would still be able to make the necessary changes as she sees fit.

You also need to find trustees to continue to administer the trust after both you and your spouse have passed on. It's good to have two contingent trustees (like my wife and I have) because circumstances can be very different in the future than the way they are right now. Perhaps that trustee is in a place where he or she can't commit to helping manage the financial assets. If there are minor children, there may be other trustees managing the money and other caregivers (sometimes called "guardians") looking after the children. So there are checks and balances there. It's not always a good thing to have one trustee manage everything (i.e., both the assets and the children) but, in some cases, there is no other solution and as long as you're confident in that trustee, he or she will be able to live up to their trustee duties.

Trustees can be friends, family, colleagues, and if you don't have an individual you can appoint, you can assign a trust department within a bank (or an independently owned trust company) to administer the trust. In that scenario, you're not going to have that personal connection and of course you'll have to pay a fee to that trust department to administer your trust. Some families decide to use a trust company instead of a family member or friend due to the possible future scenario in which an appointed trustee is not able to fulfill the duties.

When the original trustees or grantors pass away, the trust becomes irrevocable (the revocable trust can be changed at any time while the trustees are alive). You can look at the trust document as though it is a Constitution that you and the trustees have to abide by.

Always consider that you will want to give the trustee an "out" if they can't continue on with the responsibilities. So when you talk to them about this, you can say, "if something happens down the road and we're gone and you can't continue on, here's A, B, and C contacts for you to talk to after you decide you can't manage the trust anymore." If there are three trustees, for example, you will have a primary trustee, and if he or she decides they can't act as the primary trustee, the responsibility would transfer to trustee B. And if trustee B is the administrator and passes away, it then goes to trustee C, which may be the trust department of the bank or an independent trust company. There's always continuity in managing trust bylaws.

Estate Taxes

Once a final estate exceeds a certain threshold, there could be an estate tax, often referred to as a death tax. The federal estate tax exemption for 2015 is $5,430,000. What that basically means is that anything over that threshold may be exposed to an estate tax, which is currently set at 40 percent and must be paid within nine months.

Trust Alternating Distribution Provisions

Inside of a living trust, you can lay out specific requirements regarding what conditions the trust's beneficiaries must meet in order to receive funds from the trust. This is sometimes called an "incentive trust," but basically you are specifying alternatives for distributing trust assets.

Here is how my wife and I have structured our living trust: We have three young children. My wife and I feel that, as long as we are around, we are blessed with the opportunity to be able to teach our children what matters most in life and how we value life. We can coach them and help them become the best they can be. But if my wife and I are hurt in an accident or we have passed away prematurely and we haven't had that time to teach them what's most important in life, I would like our money to be used as a "carrot" as our kids grow older because they need to be mature in order to adequately deal with money. If they become more financially responsible while my wife and I are alive, we can always ease up on the guidelines of our trusts.

But while our children are still very young and impressionable, we would rather control our money in a way that we feel is an incentive for them to reach their full potential. What we have done is legally title everything that we can in the living trust. Our cars, our home, our brokerage account, our checking account, everything is in the name of the trust except our IRAs and 401(k)s (remember, IRAs and 401(k)s cannot be held inside a trust). But, nonetheless, the trust guidelines are very liberal in providing our kids everything that they would need financially in their childhood—from addressing how to buy a car when they turn 16 to having their education paid for. We also have provided our caregivers and those who would be the guardians of our children an annual stipend to help them take care of the financial burden of caregiving.

After the children graduate from college, they would have to start participating in what my wife and I feel is an appropriate adult life. In other words, they would not receive a lump sum payout as they would if they received everything through a will. If you leave everything in a will to minor children, once they turn 18, those dollars are theirs and they can potentially do whatever they want with it. Many who are 18 are not financially mature enough to manage money and often they end up squandering most of it. Sometimes, those dollars create a negative habit, perpetually prohibiting them from reaching their maximum potential. That is why my wife and I have decided that everything is staying in the trust and, if something happens to us, once the kids graduate from college, they will submit their W-2s or their 1099s to the trustee at the end of every year. We have set it up that as long as our children submit their W-2 or 1099 they will get a dollar-for-dollar match from the trust. If they decide not to work, that's okay, but they're not going to have our money to fund that lifestyle.

Before my wife and I had our three kids, she taught elementary school, and we feel that teachers today are underpaid. So we included in our trust that if any of our children decide to become teachers, they will get a two-for-one match. So, if they make $40,000 as a teacher, when they submit their W-2 at the end of the year, the trust will pay them $80,000. You can even set up your trust to require your children to do a certain number of hours a year of community service, and you can even make drug-testing mandatory prior to being eligible to take money out of the trust.

This type of customization should really only be done by attorneys who specialize in estate planning. You can be your own financial engineer as well as an engineer for your children if you align yourself with an estate planning attorney who understands your objectives.

KEY INSIGHTS FROM THIS CHAPTER

- Estate planning, in its simplest form, could be defined as how you want to transfer your "stuff" after you've passed away.
- Every adult has something they want to pass down— sometimes it is only their values, not their valuables; sometimes it is both their values and their valuables.
- Every individual, regardless of net worth, should have three documents: (1) a last will and testament, (2) a durable power of attorney, and (3) a living will.

- A last will and testament is used to distribute property to beneficiaries, specify last wishes, and name guardians for minor children. Without this document, the Probate Court will make these important decisions for you.
- Having a durable power of attorney means you're authorizing someone to act on your behalf until the day you pass away.
- A living will states whether you would like to be resuscitated or if you are want to be kept alive in a vegetative state.
- You might also want to create an "ethical will"—or a love letter that expresses your sentiments and values—to those you leave behind. This is not a legally binding document but more of a supplemental document (or video) you create to help those you leave behind.
- The more someone has to give away after their passing, especially if there are businesses involved or minor children, the more they may need a living trust.
- A living trust can be the owner of almost all your assets. When appropriately titled in the name of the trust, assets in the trust do not have to go through the probate system.
- Inside of a living trust, you can lay out specific requirements regarding what conditions the trust's beneficiaries must meet in order to receive funds from the trust.
- A living will (health-care directive) and a living trust (asset directive) are not the same thing.
- If an estate is likely to exceed certain thresholds, many things can be done to lower a couple's overall net worth so they don't have undue exposure to estate taxes—and all while doing good for humanity.

Chapter 9

Do You Need a Financial Planner?

Today, cars and smartphones are equipped with state-of-the-art GPS navigation systems. All you have to do is provide the appropriate coordinates and it will deliver you a real-time road map that will take a lot of the guesswork out of driving somewhere new.

Similar advanced technologies now exist for the financial planning industry. Having a navigation system on your retirement plan allows you to focus on the end game and not on the minutiae. A big part of having the appropriate Money Mindset is knowing where you want to go and why. That's what this book is about: (1) helping you formulate your financial road map, and (2) helping you calculate the most appropriate way to get there. Once you have that figured out, and you have an effective way of monitoring your progress, you should be able to focus on what's important in life and not get so caught up in the what-ifs of life.

Do You Need Help?

Now that you know what is required to create and effectively manage an appropriate Money Mindset in the 21st century, you have come to a financial crossroad. From here you can decide to either manage your money on your own or get professional help. In order to manage your money on your own, you will need to greatly further your education on the details and technical aspects of finances, as well as get a good understanding of global economics.

Do you have the time and energy to manage everything on your own? Are you able to manage your emotions when it comes to financial uncertainty? Are you comfortable with the daily risk and responsibility?

A March 2014 Vanguard research paper titled "Putting a Value on Your Value: Quantifying Vanguard Advisor's Alpha" concluded that if a financial planner thoroughly goes through the process and helps an individual with their asset allocation, provides behavioral coaching, and helps with their spending strategy, the advisor can add about 3 percent a year in net returns to the client's portfolio.[1] This finding may help you make your decision about whether or not to work with a qualified financial planner.

If you do choose the path to work with a financial planner, I encourage you to get to know their process of working with clients. Each advisor will have their own style and specialty but overall, they should incorporate a holistic process: engaging, exploring, designing, implementing, and managing your personal plan.

The first step in a holistic retirement planning process is *engaging* with you. The financial planner should get to know you and understand the financial "whys" of your life. In addition, data should begin to be incorporated to help you to envision the appropriate game plan to achieve your various financial goals.

Your retirement age, desired monthly income, and risk tolerance should be discussed in great detail.

Step two of the process requires the financial planner to reflect on your situation and begin to *explore* and formulate a strategic game plan that can realistically be achieved. Calculations of how much you should be investing on a monthly basis, what average rate of return is appropriate, as well as the appropriate mix of various investment vehicles are all taken into consideration.

The third step involves the financial planner showing you the potential *design* and discussing the nuances of how the plan could be implemented. Expectations of the success of the plan are discussed and all questions pertaining to the plan are answered.

The fourth step, *implementation*, takes place only when you feel comfortable with the design. This is also the stage at which the discussion takes place regarding how the assets are managed and how often you will meet with the financial planner. The implementation step is when the necessary paperwork is filled out, assets are transferred, and then funds are allocated based on the agreed design.

The last step is the day-to-day *management* of the plan and the investments within the plan. There should be a process outlining how the financial planner plans on managing the assets and how often he or she will meet with you. It is advisable to meet with your financial planner at least annually, if not more often if the need arises.

It is true, there are a lot of moving parts to the holistic retirement planning process, but if you go through it with a qualified professional and you feel that you are both on the same page, then you will be able to stop worrying that you potentially miscalculated, took on too little risk, or are overly exposed to a major economic crisis. Someone else who knows you and your financial situation is taking care of those concerns for you.

The great value of a qualified financial planner in the 21st century is that he or she can help frame your Money Mindset, guide you through the holistic retirement planning process, and hold your hand through the daily gyrations of our capitalist system. Having someone that understands your needs, wants, and wishes, and works with you regularly to accomplish your goals is quite powerful.

Truth be told, sometimes I feel more like a psychologist than a financial planner. The emotional component for my clients as I guide them to build and live off their wealth in this ever-changing economic climate can be enormous.

So how do you go about finding the right financial planner; where do you look? I believe the best way to find a competent financial planner is by a referral from a trusted source. Think about the people in your life you respect—what they've created financially, their attitudes about money, and the way they respect money. Ask them if they work with a financial planner and if they do, ask if they are satisfied with him or her and if that advisor is taking on new clients.

Another option is to utilize the Financial Planning Association's resource center, located online at www.plannersearch.org/Pages/Home.aspx.

Your Financial Education

The premise of this book isn't to teach you everything you need to know about wealth management—it is just the first step of your financial education. I hope this book will lead to further discussions among you and your colleagues, or your family and friends, or if you're currently pursuing an advanced education, that it sparks discussions in classes as well. This book hopefully gives you good ideas on how to further your financial education in specific areas and what steps you can take now to start putting together a solid financial plan. My hope is that it helps you develop the right financial mindset to harvest enough economic energy to have the financial independence that you desire.

Note

1. F. M. Kinniry, Jr., C. M. Jaconetti, M. A. DiJoseph, and Y. Zilbering, "Putting a Value on Your Value: Quantifying Vanguard Advisor's Alpha," Vanguard, https://advisors.vanguard.com/iwe/pdf/ISGQVAA .pdf?cbdForceDomain=true.

Appendix

Economic Energy

When I first started this project, the idea was to begin the book with the history and future of energy in the United States. My thought was to describe the importance of why and how North America is working toward energy independence. I would then parlay that mindset of becoming "energy independent" into the importance of becoming "financially independent."

This concept inspired the rest of the book. As I was writing it, I could imagine many of my closest confidantes asking "Why do you want to start a personal finance book with the history of energy?" I began to ask myself that same question. . . .

Once John Wiley & Sons signed on as my publisher, the direction of the book made a major shift. In the end, I feel that the final manuscript of *Money Mindset* better reflects my philosophy of money than the book *Economic Energy* could have shown.

That being said, I do think it's valuable to share the origins of this book. Here is a condensed version of the first two chapters of *Economic Energy*.

The History and Future of Energy in the United States

Scientists and sovereign nations tend to agree that energy can be viewed as both leverage and currency. Leverage in the sense that energy powers the machines of industry, enabling us to produce more, and produce it more quickly and efficiently than we could if we were reliant solely on human-powered labor. Since energy is used to create the tangible goods that drive the economy, it is currency in the sense that when all else is stripped away we are left with the conclusion that energy is the currency that underpins the entire global economic system.

This is not a new idea. In fact, in his 1981 book *Critical Path*, American neo-futuristic architect, systems theorist, author, designer, and inventor Buckminster Fuller proposed a one-world currency based not on any arbitrary unit of measure, but equal to one kilowatt-hour of electricity. As with so many of his ideas, this one was far ahead of its time, yet we are no closer to realizing his dream than we were when he first penned the book. Nonetheless, the central truth contained in his writing remains, and the idea resonates with many, even to this day.

More specifically, energy comes in two basic forms. Broadly these are "renewable" and "nonrenewable." Beneath each of these two major categories are specific energy forms. For much of the history of the United States, our energy story has been one of the extraction and use of nonrenewable forms and sources of energy, or "stuff from the ground"—coal, oil, natural gas, and, during our colonial period, wood. More recently, renewable energies have been added to the story (solar, wind, microhydro, biodiesel, biogas, and others). It could well be argued that we always have had a certain, small-scale reliance on renewables, but it has been only in recent years that they have truly come into their own.

Arc of Development in the United States

The story of the current state of energy in the United States begins in 1859 in what had been, to that point, the sleepy little town of Titusville, Pennsylvania. That's where the first U.S. oil gusher was discovered, and it unleashed America's first oil boom, which lasted from 1859 to the 1870s. Prior to the discovery at Titusville, America's cities were largely powered by coal. Those living in rural America, which was most of the population in those days, got their energy from burning wood. Some even still used whale blubber as fuel for lamps when they could not get kerosene (due to low supply or higher cost).

Titusville changed all that. Overnight, we had a new, magical, seemingly endless source of energy to tap into—and tap into it we did. It not only fueled the Pennsylvania oil boom, but ushered in an era of "wildcatting" (an exploratory process of groups or individuals prospecting for oil in new areas) that has not been replicated anywhere else since. No telling of this period would be complete without mentioning the important milestone that occurred in 1870 in Ohio: the founding of a small refining company by a man named John D. Rockefeller and a small group of other investors. The company was called Standard Oil, and until it was forcibly dissolved in 1911 due to new antitrust laws, it led and shaped the development of the oil industry, not just in the United States, but the world over. At the point of its dissolution, it was estimated that Standard Oil controlled in excess of 80 percent of the oil flows in the United States.[1]

But, as exciting as the Titusville find was, it can't be marked as the birth of the modern oil industry, or America's committed foray into it. That distinction goes to a place called Spindletop, a field near Beaumont, Texas, where a gusher of a size never before seen was discovered on January 10, 1901.[2] This particular oil find was so productive that it caused oil prices to plummet from $2 per barrel to just $0.03 as its output glutted the market—demonstrating the economic principle of supply and demand. However, it didn't take long for our enterprising nation to find ever more uses for the new "black gold," and those prices quickly recovered. From there, the hunt was officially on, and the wildcatting phenomenon that swept across the continent was every bit as exciting and dynamic as the gold rushes our nation had seen before.

Then, in 1908 Henry Ford introduced the Model T. That was when the consumption of crude oil really started to accelerate. Previously, automobiles were wildly expensive luxuries, but now the average working American could afford to buy a car. Ford revolutionized the automobile industry by learning how to make a lot more cars, for a lot less money, in a lot less time. His innovation? The moving assembly line. Affordable cars changed American society and American lives. The demand for the Model T became so strong that we soon became addicted to crude oil to feed our appetites for automobiles.

Discoveries in the Middle East

Oil was first discovered in the Middle East in 1908 in Persia, or what is today the nation of Iran. These new discoveries sent global production levels ever higher, and the industrializing Western world was ever hungrier for its output—so much so that Middle Eastern exploration continued unabated by the companies spun off after the breakup of Standard Oil, as well as a number of European companies. Like Spindletop in Texas, the Middle East's defining moment was the discovery of the virtually limitless oil fields of Saudi Arabia in 1938. This was a turning point for the oil industry, and what made it a truly global phenomenon.

It is also important to understand that the oil produced belonged to the companies that did the work of drilling it and shipping it off to refineries. Yes, the countries from which the oil was extracted were paid for their resource, but the lion's share of the profits went to the Western companies who were handling the logistics of pulling it from the ground. This was true for two reasons. The first was simple pragmatism and business. The second reason is that, by and large, the population of the Middle East lacked the expertise and engineering skills to extract the oil.

When the Ottoman Empire (historically referred to as the Turkish Empire or Turkey) was sundered in 1922, vast swaths of the Middle East were colonized by various European powers. Their lands were no longer their own, and neither were the immense resources they contained. That, combined with the aforementioned lack of technical skill to extract the raw materials, made it a given that the countries with oil resources were largely shut out of the profits realized from its extraction.

And it was extracted. By the end of World War I, demand for oil was surging, prompting ever greater investments in any area that was likely to contain oil reserves. Given the previous finds in Persia, the three Ms—men, materials, and money—poured into the region to explore and extract whatever could be found. Now we are historically at a point where most readers are likely to be familiar with the events. Everyone knows the results of those explorations. They led to some of the largest oil finds in history, and as they did, Western companies gained an ever-tighter stranglehold on Middle Eastern oil.

The Rise of Nationalization

The stranglehold began to change in 1960, with the formation of the Organization of Petroleum Exporting Countries (OPEC). Previous to the formation of this group, Iran (formerly Persia) led the charge and nationalized its oil resources, summarily throwing out the Western companies and taking command of its own resources. The formation OPEC laid the groundwork for others to follow, and they did. Iraq nationalized its reserves in 1961, Burma and Egypt in 1962, Argentina and Indonesia in 1963, and Peru in 1968.

Overwhelmingly, the reason cited for the drive toward the nationalization of oil resources was exploitation by the West, and although it took OPEC a number of years to find its footing and get itself organized, given the hostile climate and the wave of nationalization that followed its formation, it was only a matter of time before it led to a showdown. Having gained control over their national resources, and knowing full well that the West had come to rely increasingly on Middle Eastern oil, the day inevitably came when the Middle Eastern countries sought to use their rising economic power as a heavy club.

The Embargo Period

To understand what specifically led to the 1973 Oil Embargo, it is important to note three international events. First, in 1970 U.S. oil production peaked. When it did, the United States became ever more dependent on Middle Eastern oil to meet its insatiable appetite. Second, on October 6, 1973, the Yom Kippur war began, wherein a number of Arab states banded together to launch a surprise attack on an unprepared Israel in an attempt to push the nation of Israel into the sea. In this, they were spectacularly unsuccessful, and despite being hopelessly outnumbered, Israel prevailed against them. Third, and perhaps most important, on October 12, 1973, in response to a Russian treaty arming the Middle East against Israel, the United States began airlifting weapons and supplies to that beleaguered nation.

Seeking to punish the United States for its pro-Israel stance, OPEC banded together and issued an embargo. It was this action that prompted President Nixon to take his message to the people of America. In that message, he went on television to promise the American people energy "independence" within 10 years. Needless to say, we didn't come close to reaching that goal.

The reality was that the Oil Embargo proved to be an effective weapon in the short run. The recession it caused in the United States was notably sharp and painful, but certainly not debilitating. In the long term, though, its success has been debatable. Although the United States did not succeed in its quest for energy independence in a decade, the embargo did redouble U.S. efforts to find alternate sources for the fuels necessary to power its industries. Those sources were systematically found and developed, leading to additional discoveries worldwide, including many within the borders of the United States itself. The cumulative impact of those discoveries, along with improvements in technology that made previously inaccessible oil resources obtainable, eroded the power of OPEC. This is not to say that they are utterly without power. OPEC nations still command an enormous chunk of global oil production but, based on current trends, the United States is on track to become the world's largest oil producer, moving ahead of both Russia and Saudi Arabia by 2015.[3]

Current Trends

In recent years, we've seen another emerging trend that is every bit as important as those that have come before. China's entry into the solar panel market has dramatically reduced prices. In many parts of the country, solar energy is competitive with, and often cheaper than, energy from coal-fired power plants. This is leading to a revolution unlike any the energy industry in the United States has seen to date.

According to one of the world's leading inventors, Ray Kurzweil, all of the world's energy needs can be met with 1/10,000th of the sunlight that hits the Earth each day.

Specifically, solar energy is leading to a decentralization of energy production. With solar, individuals are now empowered, they have all the tools they need to see to their own energy production. They can be, if they wish, energy independent. On the whole, state-level governments have embraced this new paradigm, with 43 of them signing net-metering laws to date. The significance of this cannot be understated: Net metering allows individuals to stay connected to the centralized power grid, while generating some fraction of their total power needs. In months where they produce more energy than they need personally, they can sell their excess power back to the grid and draw from it during times when their individual output is insufficient to provide 100 percent of the power they need.

The central grid then, acts as a giant battery, removing the necessity for individuals to invest in expensive battery banks to provide power during periods of low panel output. The battery backup system has historically been the single-most expensive component of a private solar power system, and that fact, coupled with the impact of Chinese industrial, might lower the per unit cost of panels, has created a significant paradigm shift.

Finally, one cannot examine current energy trends in the United States without giving a nod to Elon Musk. Tesla automobiles are arguably the best cars ever made, and Musk has not only delivered the Holy Grail of all electric cars, with a staggering 200+ miles per charge range, but has also single-handedly built a network of charging stations that span from one end of the country to the other.

In looking at the energy landscape now and in the future, these factors cannot be ignored. Simply put, the more deeply entrenched these new technologies become in our economy, the less we'll have to use the finite resources we are extracting from the ground. That, in turn, provides a one-two punch that puts the United States firmly on course for the energy independence we have been seeking for more than four decades.

U.S. energy independence relates to the goal of reducing U.S. imports of oil and other foreign sources of energy. Being energy independent means that the United States will be unaffected by global energy supply disruptions due to politically unstable countries and/or other macroeconomic issues. (It is easy to see the parallel between oil resources and the money resources in your own life, and how being financially independent removes the worries that come from being reliant on a job or business enterprise, isn't it?)

Energy Forecast for North America

When speaking of energy independence, it is unlikely that the United States will achieve total energy independence on its own. If North America could achieve energy independence, and given that the United States is far and away the largest economy in North America, that would offer the same benefits as national energy independence. There are many forces converging that are making this outcome ever more likely. Let's discuss some of these forces.

Oil and Natural Gas

Two things are driving the current U.S. energy boom: the lifting of the moratorium of offshore drilling and shale. Shale provides the United States with both oil and natural gas in abundance. In fact, the United States has been called the "Saudi Arabia of natural gas" for good reason.[4] We've known the locations of the major formations for decades, but it has only been recently, through modern technology, that we've been able to squeeze the oil and natural gas from the land.

Entrepreneur George Mitchell pioneered the horizontal drilling technique called fracking (hydraulic fracturing). The technique includes drilling down (sometimes miles), turning horizontally, and injecting water and sand under pressure to force the release of natural gas from layers of rock. The technique can even rejuvenate existing oil wells.

While fracking may sound great at first, there are some potential environmental issues, including the risk of earthquakes, extraordinary use of water, and the potential of polluting aquifers. *Gasland* (2010) by Josh Fox is a fairly damaging documentary that showed the iconic image of a person holding a lighter up to their tap water and igniting it. It was shocking, to say the least. These concerns are, by and large, overplayed in the media. This is not to say that they aren't legitimate, and they are being addressed, but these improvements are being done in tandem with extraction, rather than halting extraction until the issues are fully addressed.

As the images clearly illustrate, we have barely scratched the surface in terms of shale extraction of oil and natural gas. This isn't a short-term boom, but the beginning of a very long era of renewed resource extraction in the United States.

The results of this new flurry of activity are allowing the United States to import less foreign oil and natural gas. This is proof that we are increasingly coming to rely on our own resources to meet our energy needs.

OPEC's Mistake

Doug Cote, Chief Market Strategist with Voya Investment Management, has this to say about OPEC's future: "By choosing to ignore Econ 101, the Organization of Petroleum Exporting Countries (OPEC) sowed the seeds of its own destruction. Persistently high oil prices inspired the U.S. energy renaissance, as oil-path entrepreneurs married age-old drilling techniques with modern technology to launch the most unexpected and successful supply side shock in a generation—supply that would not have been feasible at lower oil prices. We expect drilling technology will continue to improve apace, increasing output, lowering costs, and putting the OPEC cartel—a myopic and monolithic monopoly—out of business."

What Our Emerging Independence Means for Manufacturing

North America's emerging energy independence has cast-off effects as well. In addition to the effect of growth in global supplies pushing prices lower, our total energy costs will continue to be lower than those of our competitor nations around the world, making the United States an increasingly attractive manufacturing location. North America's energy independence will make the United States an attractive place to manufacture goods and to build service companies.

Let's not forget that for decades, the United States suffered the effects of offshoring. Millions of manufacturing jobs disappeared from our shores. Happily, those jobs are in the very beginning stages of returning now, thanks to our highly competitive labor force and our low energy costs.

Global Impacts

On one hand, it would be tempting to say that the surge in U.S. oil production would hurt the economies of the trading partners from whom we currently import large amounts of oil. Indeed, at first glance, the numbers would lend the appearance of a very large negative impact.

Oil Exports to United States as Percentage of Domestic GDP
- Angola: 8.1 percent (2012)
- Nigeria: 6.6 percent (2011)
- Kuwait: 4.4 percent (2010)
- Saudi Arabia: 8.3 percent (2011)

- Iraq: 4.5 percent (2010)
- Canada: 5.7 percent (2012)
- Mexico: 4 percent (2012)[5]

To provide some context for these figures, when the United States suffered through the Great Recession from 2007 to 2009, our GDP contracted by 7.6 percent annualized.[6] To say that the results were unpleasant is an understatement, so you can see by looking at the numbers above that if the United States were to suddenly stop importing from these nations, the hit to their respective economies would be dire. On the other hand, it is unlikely that the United States would ever completely stop importing at least some of its oil, but with surging production of our own, we could certainly be more strategic about it. We absolutely would not have to rely on Middle Eastern oil, and could content ourselves primarily with imports from North America and/or valued strategic partners around the world. Even then, though, the consequences to those we stopped buying from would not be as dire as the figures above might lead you to believe. In the first place, the United States wouldn't simply cut off all imports overnight. It would be a gradual drawdown that would likely take a number of years to play out. Secondly, the burgeoning economies of China and India are resource starved, and with their combined population some seven times greater than our own, they would quickly fill the gap in demand that the United States left. It could possibly play out like this: As the United States increasingly withdrew from the global oil market, prices would inevitably begin to fall. As prices fell, it would create more opportunities for cash-strapped entrepreneurs in China and India to make investments, relying on cheap oil to fuel their enterprises. In the medium term, this would cause prices to rise again, and these newly formed companies could pay the increase in price because they would be turning a profit at that point. The net effect then would be nominal, although there would be some pains for these nations as exports to the United States began to drop off and prices dipped.

In the time since I began writing *Economic Energy*, the price of oil has dropped from $100 (July 2014) to $52 (February 2015).

Renewable Energy

The utilization of fossil fuels will continue to be the primary source of electricity for the United States for the foreseeable future. See the table shown here. With that being said, the world is beginning to explore different ways to harness renewable energy.

U.S. Electricity Production by Source

39%	Coal
27%	Natural gas
19%	Nuclear
6%	Hydropower
1.7%	Biomass
0.4%	Geothermal
0.4%	Solar
4.4%	Wind
1%	Petroleum
<1%	Other gases

SOURCE: U.S Energy Information Administration. Data as of 2014.

Solar Power

Of all the renewables, solar offers the biggest, best, and brightest potential in the long term. There are a number of new or emerging technologies making solar ever more attractive. The United States has 43 gigawatts (1 billion watts = 1 gigawatt) of solar plants either currently being built or in the planning stages. Germany just crossed an important threshold and is now generating 31 percent of its base load electrical needs from renewable resources like solar and wind.[7]

The beautiful thing about solar, aside from the fact that we'll never run out of it, is that its impact can be felt both at the level of centralized power supply (power plants) and decentralized power supply (individuals installing their own systems). Taken together, these provide a powerful one-two punch that is making solar increasingly hard to ignore.

When you factor in the continuing efficiency improvements in solar panels, and new advances in cheap, high-capacity battery storage, it seems clear that solar could play an increasingly important role in both our overall energy mix, and in our bid for energy independence.

Despite our vast oil reserves and deposits of shale, eventually those finite resources could run out. The more we can come to rely on renewables, the less likely the chance of exhausting our finite resources.

Other Alternative Energy

There is no shortage of alternate energy ideas on the market today. There are high-efficiency wind turbines, great for rural areas, and especially well suited for the American Midwest; biogas reactors, which are, again, particularly well suited to rural areas; biodiesel production, especially from waste oil and algae reactors; and, most important, low-flow microhydro generators, which are small and affordable devices that individuals can buy and place in running water to generate electricity for themselves. Even with the dramatically lower price of solar power these days, the biggest, most efficient means of personal energy production is in the area of micro-hydro, but of course, that's only true if you live next to a stream or river. Micro-hydro is effective, but self-limiting.

Nonetheless, all of these technologies have a role to play in our energy future, and increasingly, the people of the United

States are realizing that taking a small measure of control over their own energy production is extremely empowering and liberating.

The Big Picture

The facts are undeniable. The United States is on its way to virtual energy independence. Our vast shale resources, a renewed interest in off-shore drilling, and increasingly competitive prices in solar are the trio of pillars supporting this new possibility.

In 1973, President Richard Nixon spoke of attempting to achieve American energy independence. The words he spoke were meant to evoke the same level of excitement and enthusiasm as Kennedy's "We choose to go to the moon" speech more than a decade earlier.

Here is what President Nixon said, after asking for Americans to universally make sacrifices in energy consumption due to the Oil embargo crisis:

> Let me conclude by restating our overall objective. It can be summed up in one word that best characterizes this Nation and its essential nature. That word is "independence." From its beginning 200 years ago, throughout its history, America has made great sacrifices of blood and also of treasure to achieve and maintain its independence. In the last third of this century, our independence will depend on maintaining and achieving self-sufficiency in energy.

For the first time since 1974, the goal to achieve energy independence is in our sights. We have the technology, infrastructure, market forces, and capital incentives for entrepreneurs to reach our respectable goal.

Notes

1. Keith Poole, "Biography: John D. Rockefeller, Senior," *American Experience* series, www.pbs.org/wgbh/americanexperience/features/biography/rockefellers-john/.
2. "Historical Timeline: History of Alternative Energy and Fossil Fuels," ProCon.org, http://alternativeenergy.procon.org/view.timeline.php?timelineID=000015#1900-1950.
3. "The Road to Energy Independence" (Infographic), Oilprice.com Editorial Department, http://oilprice.com/Finance/investing-and-trading-reports/The-R2woad-to-Energy-Independence-Info-graphic.html.
4. Jason Koebler, "Obama: U.S. 'Saudi Arabia of Natural Gas,'" *U.S. News & World Report*, January 26, 2012, www.USnews.com/news/articles/2012/01/26/obama-US-saudi-arabia-of-natural-gas.
5. Richard Anderson, "How American Energy Independence Could Change the World," BBC News, April 3, 2014, www.bbc.com/news/business-23151813.
6. Bob Willis, "U.S. Recession Worst Since Great Depression, Revised Data Show," Bloomberg, August 1, 2009, www.bloomberg.com/apps/news?pid=newsarchive&sid=aNivTjr852TI.
7. Caroline Winter, "Germany Reaches New Levels of Greendom, Gets 31 Percent of Its Electricity from Renewables," Bloomberg Business, August 14, 2014, www.bloomberg.com/bw/articles/2014-08-14/germany-reaches-new-levels-of-greendom-gets-31-percent-of-its-electricity-from-renewables.

Glossary

72(t) A section in the Internal Revenue Code that provides guidelines for early withdrawals from retirement-based accounts.

401(k) A type of qualified, employer-based plan in which employees can set aside a portion of their before-tax earnings for retirement. Account balances grow tax deferred until retirement, at which time distributions are taxed as ordinary income. Some employers offer their employees a match for a percentage of their contributions.

403(b) A type of qualified retirement based plan that is established by a nonprofit or a public-education organization. Employees can set aside a portion of their before-tax earnings for retirement. Account balances grow tax deferred until retirement, at which time distributions are taxed as ordinary income.

457 plan A type of qualified deferred compensation plan that is established by a state or a local government. Employees can set aside a portion of their before-tax earnings for retirement. Account balances grow tax deferred until retirement, at which time distributions are taxed as ordinary income.

adjusted gross income (AGI) An income tax term commonly used to refer to the taxpayer's gross income less specified expenses, such as traditional IRA and employer-sponsored retirement plan contributions.

agent A person licensed by a state (or states) to sell insurance.

annual percentage rate (APR) The annual rate that is charged for borrowing, expressed as a single percentage number that represents the actual yearly cost of funds over the term of the loan.

annual percentage yield (APY) The effective annual rate of return, taking into account the effect of compound interest.

asset allocation The process of dividing investments among different asset classes to optimize the risk/reward trade-off.

asset allocation funds Mutual funds that offer a one-stop fund that includes U.S. stocks, international stocks, government bonds, corporate bonds, money-market accounts, and real estate markets.

asset classes Different categories of investments that include domestic stocks, international stocks, government bonds, corporate bonds, and real estate.

balanced funds Mutual funds that maintain a balanced combination of common stocks, bonds, and perhaps preferred stocks. Balanced funds offer both income and growth because they hold both bonds and stocks.

bearish A term that is used to express a negative investment attitude.

bear market A prolonged decline in stock prices that extends over a period of time. A 20 percent decline in value is a generally accepted indication of a bear market.

beneficiary The person who receives benefits or payments from an estate or an insurance policy.

blue-chip stocks Corporations with some of the highest quality of all common stocks because they are dominant companies that have the ability to pay steady dividends in both good and bad times.

bond A debt instrument that is issued by a government, state, city, municipality, or corporation. The seller of the bond agrees to repay the original principal amount of the loan at a specified time and agrees to make scheduled interest payments.

bond rating A measurement of quality and safety pertaining to the issuer's financial condition. In other words, an evaluation from a rating agency that indicates the likelihood of the debt issuer's ability to meet scheduled interest and principal repayments. Ratings range from AAA (highest quality) to D (lowest quality).

bullish A term that is used to express an optimistic investment attitude.

bull market A prolonged advance in stock prices that extends over a period of time. A 20 percent increase in value is a generally accepted indication of a bull market.

cash-flow planning The management of the inflows and outflows of a person's day-to-day income.

cash value The equity (savings) component within certain life insurance policies.

certificate of deposit (CD) A short-term deposit through a financial institution that pays a specific interest rate for a specific period of time.

claim A demand made by the insured, or the insured's beneficiary, for payment of benefits provided by an insurance policy.

Consumer Credit Protection (Truth in Lending) Act A federal law that allows individuals the ability to properly compare credit terms from all lending institutions in order to make meaningful comparisons.

convertible bond funds These funds are bonds or preferred stock that can be exchanged for a fixed number of shares in the common stock of the issuing company. Convertible bond funds combine features of both stocks and bonds.

convertible bonds A corporate bond that can be converted into stock at a predetermined price.

corporate bond funds Mutual funds that diversify their holdings in various forms of corporate debt.

corporate bonds A debt instrument that is issued by a corporation and sold to investors. The backing for the bond is usually the payment ability of the company.

coupon The interest rate stated on a bond when it's issued. The coupon is typically paid semiannually.

cyclical stocks Companies whose earnings tend to fluctuate sharply with their business's cycles.

debt instrument Also known as a bond. *See* bond.

deductible The amount of an insured loss paid by the policyholder. If you have a $500 deductible for auto insurance, you pay the first $500 worth of damages to your car if you are in an accident. As deductibles increase, premiums decrease.

defensive stocks Companies that are considered to be recession resistant. They often sell products, such as items that a person eats, drinks, or smokes in all types of economies.

deferred compensation plan A type of employer-sponsored retirement plan where compensation has been earned by the employee but has not yet been paid from the employer. With total direction from the employee, the employer holds the income, invests it, and delays the payment for a set period of time that defers the taxation of the income.

defined–benefit plan A type of employer-sponsored retirement plan where lifetime retirement income is provided for the employee through the use of various formula-based models (salary history and duration of employment). The responsibility of contributions, investment risk, and portfolio management is with the employer.

disability insurance An insurance policy that provides supplementary income in the event of an illness or accident resulting in a disability that prevents the insured from working.

diversification The spreading of risk by placing assets in various types of investments.

dividend A distribution of a portion of a company's earnings, decided by the board of directors, to a class of its shareholders.

dollar cost averaging An investment method that involves regular and routine purchases of a security of equal dollar amounts.

Dow Jones Industrial Average (DJIA) A price-weighted American index that measures the share price of 30 industrial-based corporations.

durable power of attorney A legal document giving one person the power to act for another person, even if the individual becomes incapacitated.

earnings per share The total amount of earning divided by the number of shares outstanding.

equity-income funds Mutual funds that seek a portfolio of high-dividend paying stocks, convertible securities, and bonds.

estate The value of items that an individual owns, such as stocks, bonds, real estate, art collections, collectibles, antiques, jewelry, life insurance, and anything else of value.

estate tax A federal tax levied on an heir's inherited portion of an estate if the value of the estate exceeds an exclusion limit set by law. The estate tax does not apply to surviving spouses.

exchange-traded funds (ETFs) An index fund that trades like a stock.

exclusions Specific situations, conditions, or circumstances not covered by an insurance policy.

fixed-income investment A debt instrument that pays a fixed rate of income per year until maturity.

gift tax A federal tax applied to an individual giving anything of value to another person.

global stock funds Mutual funds that specialize in corporations throughout the world, including the United States.

government bonds A debt instrument that is backed by the full faith and credit of a government. The government agrees to repay the original principal amount of the loan at a specified time and agrees to make scheduled interest payments.

government bond funds Mutual funds who own securities that are backed by the full faith and credit of a government.

grantor The creator of a trust, meaning the individual whose assets are placed into the trust.

growth and income funds Mutual funds that seek a balanced stock portfolio of growth as well as current income form dividends.

growth stocks Corporations whose earnings are reinvested in capital projects and therefore normally do not pay a dividend.

holographic will A handwritten will.

home-equity loans A type of loan in which the borrower uses the equity in their home as collateral.

income stocks Corporations where a substantial portion of earnings are paid out in the form of a dividend.

index funds Mutual funds that replicate the stocks of a broad section of the market.

inflation The rate at which the prices for goods and services are rising, and subsequently resulting in a loss of purchasing power.

insured The person/organization covered under an insurance policy.

insurer An insurance company. Also known as a carrier.

international bonds Debt instruments that are issued by corporations and/or governments outside the United States.

international bond funds Mutual funds that typically invest primarily in high-quality foreign government or corporate bonds.

international stocks Stocks of companies that are outside the United States.

international stock funds Mutual funds that specialized in companies outside the United States.

liability The responsibility for causing injury to someone or damage to property.

large cap stock A publicly traded company that has a market capitalization of $10 billion or more.

life insurance loan A loan issued by an insurance company that uses the cash value of a person's life insurance policy as collateral.

liquidity The ability to convert an asset to cash quickly without affecting the asset's price. Also known as "marketability."

living trust A trust developed by a person during his or her lifetime. Typically, it is used to maintain control over assets while alive and to control the disposition of them at death. A living trust avoids the probate process and may provide for the immediate distribution of assets.

living will A legal document that sets the guidelines for the medical care an individual desires in the event that he or she becomes incapacitated.

long-term growth funds Mutual funds that seek capital gains from companies that have potential for steady growth in earnings. Less volatile, and more consistent than maximum capital gains funds, growth funds aim to achieve a rate of growth that beats inflation.

marketability *See* liquidity.

market capitalization The market value of a company's outstanding shares. Multiply the stock price by the total number of outstanding shares.

micro cap stock A publicly traded company that has a market capitalization ranging from $50 million to $300 million.

mid cap stock A publicly traded company that has a market capitalization ranging from $2 billion to $10 billion.

money market mutual fund A mutual fund that invests primarily in short-term financial instruments such as Treasury bills and CDs.

mortgage-backed security An investment that represents pools of mortgages backed by a specific government agency.

municipal bond A debt security that is issued by a municipality, state, or county to finance its capital expenditures. The interest is exempt from federal taxes and from most state and local taxes if you live in the state in which the bond is issued.

mutual fund A diversified, professionally managed portfolio of securities that pools the assets of investors and invests in accordance with a stated set of objectives.

policyholder A person/organization that purchases an insurance policy.

precious metal funds Mutual funds that primarily invest in stocks of gold-mining firms and other companies engaged in the business of precious metals.

premium The amount of money paid or payable for coverage under an insurance policy.

price/earnings ratio (P/E ratio) A company's current share price divided by the per-share earnings.

probate The legal process in which a will is reviewed to determine whether it is valid and authentic.

qualified retirement plan A type of employer-based retirement plan that provides a tax benefit when employees contribute.

rate The cost of a unit of insurance; the basis for the premium.

real rate of return The return on an investment expressed as a percentage after subtracting the effects of taxes and inflation.

refinancing The restructuring of debt that incorporates a change to the number of years until maturity and/or the interest rate of the loan.

required minimum distribution (RMD) An annual amount that qualified plan participants must distribute from their pre-tax retirement accounts once they turn 70½ years of age.

risk The possibility of loss. The chance that an investment's actual return will be different than expected.

risk tolerance The degree of uncertainty that an investor can handle in regards to the valuation of their investment.

Roth IRA An individual retirement account that is funded with after-tax dollars and grows income-tax free. Unlike traditional IRA accounts, a Roth IRA does not require you to take a minimum distribution at a specific age.

savings incentive match plans for employees (SIMPLE plan) An employer sponsored plan under which plan contributions are made to participating employee's IRA. Tax-deferred contribution levels are higher than for IRAs but probably lower than SEPs.

secured loan A debt backed by collateral to reduce the risk associated with lending.

simplified employee pension plan (SEP) An employer-sponsored plan under which plan contributions are made to participating employee's IRA. These contribution amounts are usually higher than the IRA contribution.

small company growth funds Also called emerging growth funds, these are a type of maximum capital gain fund specializing in stocks of promising small companies.

small cap stock A publicly traded company that has a market capitalization ranging from $300 million to $2 billion.

socially responsible funds Mutual funds that limit their investments to companies that are not involved in or produce products that are social or morally controversial.

speculative stocks A company where it's stock price is subjected to a wider swing in share price compared to a typical stock.

Standard & Poor's 500 Stock Index An index of 500 American corporations that are considered to be an overall representation of the U.S. stock market.

stock An equity ownership position in a corporation that provides the possibility for dividends and growth.

stop-loss order An order that is placed to sell a security when it reaches a certain price.

tax-deferred savings plans A savings plan that is registered with the U.S. government and provides deferral of tax obligations until distribution.

term life insurance A life insurance policy that provides coverage for a fixed period of time. After that period, the insured can either drop the policy or pay annual premium increases to continue coverage.

testamentary trust A trust that is created as a result of explicit instructions from a deceased's will.

time horizon The length of time over which an investment is made or held before it is liquidated.

traditional IRA An individual retirement account that generally is funded with before-tax dollars and grows income tax deferred. Withdrawals are subjected to ordinary income tax and may also be subject to a 10 percent penalty if withdrawn prior to age 59½. Unlike Roth IRA accounts, a traditional IRA requires you to take minimum distributions beginning at the age of 70½.

Treasury bill A short-term debt security issued by the U.S. government that matures between 4 and 26 weeks after issue. Treasury bills are purchased at a discount and mature at their face value.

Treasury bonds A long-term debt security issued by the U.S. government that has a maturity of more than 10 years. Interest is paid semiannually and is exempt from state and local income taxes.

Treasury note A mid-term debt security issued by the U.S. government that matures in 1 to 10 years. Interest is paid semiannually and is exempt from state and local income taxes.

trust document A fiduciary relationship where one party, known as the grantor, gives another party, the trustee, the right to hold title to property or assets for the benefit of a third party, the beneficiary.

trustee An individual who holds or manages assets for the benefit of another.

underwriter An insurance company employee who reviews applications for insurance to ensure they are acceptable and appropriately priced. Sometimes this term refers to an insurer.

unsecured loan A loan that is issued and supported only by the borrower's creditworthiness, rather than by some sort of collateral.

U.S. savings bonds A bond that offers a fixed rate of interest over a fixed period of time.

variable life insurance A form of whole life insurance that allows the owner of the policy to allocate a portion of your premium dollars to a separate account comprised of various investment options.

volatility The relative rate at which the price of a security or group of securities moves up and down, often in comparison to the price movement of the S&P 500.

whole life insurance A life insurance policy that remains in force for the insured's whole life and requires premiums to be paid every year into the policy.

will A legal document that takes effect at death and indicates who is to administer an estate and how the estate is to be distributed. Wills may contain testamentary trusts as well as instructions for the care of dependents.

About the Author

Jacob H. Gold is the president of Jacob Gold & Associates, Inc., a private wealth management firm located in Scottsdale, Arizona. He and his team provide personalized, comprehensive financial guidance in the areas of retirement planning and wealth preservation.

As a third-generation wealth manager, CERTIFIED FINANCIAL PLANNER™ practitioner, and adjunct professor of finance at the W.P. Carey School of Business at Arizona State University, his understanding of financial planning and investing seems to be embedded in his DNA. He was mentored by his father and grandfather at a young age and learned the fundamentals of the flow of money, the management of money, and the psychology of money that have helped him throughout his life and career.

Gold is also a trusted source for market-related commentary and shares his knowledge with some of the largest names in the media world. In addition to his regular personal finance articles for *U.S. News & World Report* and the *Huffington Post*, he regularly shares his financial philosophies with a number of media outlets, including the *Wall Street Journal*, *USA Today*, the *New York Times*, *Newsweek*, and CNBC.

Index